Hu$$lel

Money, Ownership & Business Lessons Inspired by Nipsey Hussle + a Step by Step Guide on How to Implement Each Principle

By

Ash'Cash

First published in the United States of America.

DISCLAIMER

The advice contained in this material might not be suitable for everyone. The author designed the information to present his opinion about the subject matter. The reader must carefully investigate all aspects of any business decision before committing him or herself. The author obtained the information contained herein from sources he believes to be reliable and from his own personal experience, but he neither implies nor intends any guarantee of accuracy. The author is not in the business of giving legal, accounting, or any other type of professional advice. Should the reader need such advice, he or she must seek services from a competent professional. The author particularly disclaims any liability, loss, or risk taken by individuals who directly or indirectly act on the information contained herein. The author believes the advice presented here is sound, but readers cannot hold him responsible for either the actions they take or the risk taken by individuals who directly or indirectly act on the information contained herein.

***This book is not endorsed by the Nipsey Hussle estate, the Marathon Clothing store or any of its affiliates. The content included within is designed to provide financial and business lessons inspired by Nipsey Hussle that can empower the community"**

Published by 1BrickPublishing
A division of Ash Cash Enterprises, LLC
Printed in the United States

ISBN 978-1949303049

DEDICATION

This book is **NOT for informational purposes only!** This book is a **call to action** for those who love Nipsey Hussle, for those who connected with his music, and for those who saw and understood his vision of financial independence.

This book is also **a call to action** for those who are just being introduced to his work and are ready to follow the blueprint that he selflessly laid.

DEDICATION REQUEST

Please pass a copy of this book to anyone you care about and who is in need of a blueprint on how to live their best life. **A FREE** copy of this book will always be available at

www.Husslenomics.com

TABLE OF CONTENTS

Introduction

Long Live Nipsey Hussle

Nipsey Hussle born Ermias Joseph Asghedom is often cited as a rapper and songwriter from Los Angeles, California but he was much more than that. Nipsey was a visionary, entrepreneur, community organizer, real estate investor, cryptocurrency enthusiast, activist, mentor, he was a Superior Man in every sense of the words. Through his business moves, music, and community activism he was on a mission to teach his community about being fiscally responsible and owning your now and your future in order to build wealth.

Nipsey showed us that through patience and perseverance you can achieve all of your dreams and then some. It started with an unwavering belief in himself, his team, and his community. Where others would've given up, Nipsey stuck it out for the long run. When things seemed impossible, he pushed through and made it happen. Nipsey showed us what unconditional love for his family and his community looked like.

Nipsey was a savvy businessman who knew that the key to true financial independence was ownership. He has changed the game forever, not only for independent music artists but for any creative and/or entrepreneur who wants to enjoy the fruit of their labor. He gave us the blueprint for marketing and branding and taught us that multiple streams of income, coupled with mailbox money (passive income) are the recipe for financial abundance.

Above all, Nipsey Hussle lived by the G code! He was a man of integrity, someone with strong morals and demonstrated that he was willing to dedicate his life to make the lives of those around him and his community at large, better. His actions spoke as loud as his words and his words were prolific. He made you feel him and his authentic unapologetic nature made him a rare breed and someone you can trust is not trying to steer you wrong.

HussleNomics is a book dedicated to the legacy and teachings of Mr. Hussle with a step by step guide on how to implement each principle in your life. We begin the book with the question, "Why is Neighborhood Nip So Important?" in this chapter we discuss, what he stood for, what he was able to accomplish, and why it's still is so very important for the culture. We then dive into The Making of Nipsey Hussle and The Ghetto Economic Trap. In this chapter, we discuss the history of inner-cities in America to find the root cause of gang-culture and economic injustice. We also tap into Nipsey's upbringing to discuss how he developed his paradigm. The next chapter titled, "The Philosophy of Ermias Asghedom" goes through thirty-three "Ermiasisms" that make up the foundation of Nipsey's business and money savvy. The following chapter is a step by step guide on how to create your own victory lap, then we discuss and define many business terms that Nipsey used in his vernacular. Lastly, we give you a glimpse of his library. It is known that Nipsey was an avid reader, so we've compiled a list of the 59 books that Nip

-sey was said to have read to increase his business IQ.

Nipsey often preached about the Marathon and as you know in a marathon you often have to run the full length of the race by yourself but as you will see, Nipsey made sure he surrounded himself with a powerful team that helped him during the race. As the African proverb states, "If you want to go fast, go alone, If you want to go far then go together." Many marathons offer a relay category in which a group of runners complete the race by doing one or more legs of varying distances. Metaphorically and practically, it's time to take the baton and finish what he started! Long Live Nipsey Hussle! This is just the beginning!

1

Why is Neighborhood Nip So Important

Ermias Joseph Asghedom aka Nipsey Hussle aka Nipsey the Great aka Neighborhood Nip is one of the most important figures in the fight for financial equality everywhere. When the history books are written, Nipsey will be mentioned with the Marcus Garveys, Malcolm Xs, and Martin Luther King Jrs. who came before him. In fact, Nipsey is all three reincarnated into one but had a more powerful tool in his arsenal; music. Similar to how Bob Marley used his platform to help liberate the masses, Nipsey used the highest form of vibration to speak to the souls of men and women, especially in the inner-cities. As Martin Luther King Jr. once famously said, "Inequality for one is Inequality for all... Or was it, "Injustice for one is Injustice for all?" I was paraphrasing but what Dr. King really said was, "Injustice anywhere is a threat to justice everywhere." and what Dr. King knew and ultimately died for was that his dream had to extend further than just civil rights but also silver rights. Silver rights is a concept that documents and validates the next phase of civil rights. The overall concept is that we transition beyond giving a fish, beyond teaching to fish, to owning the pond itself.

Most people remember Dr. Martin Luther King as the civil rights icon that he was but for some reason, the mention of his economic freedom fight is rarely spoken about. Dr. King was on a mission to urge America to redistribute wealth. He knew that the rhetoric of "pulling yourself up by your bootstraps" didn't really apply to black people because many started out with no boots.

It was easy to recognize Dr. King's fight for civil rights because theoretically there was a clear start and a clear end of that struggle. Some will argue that the civil rights movement started at the Montgomery bus boycott and ended in 1965 when the Voting Rights Act was passed. In order to address economic inequality though, we have to visit a dark past that America is not really comfortable talking about. This dark past is what built America and is what systemically left many African-Americans in ghettos, distressed, and economically destitute.

Will Smith posted a poignant ideal on his Instagram a while back discussing the difference between fault and responsibility. His stance was simply that no matter whose fault it is for something happening, it is the individual who is affected that is responsible for the repair of their own life. It is also that individual who has the power to change their life for the better. This is not to say that if you are done wrong that the person or entity that has done you wrong doesn't have an obligation to make it right... but the responsibility to make yourself whole is always on you. This is the approach that Nipsey took and as he taught his world these methods, he started to not only liberate minds but also put his community in a position to exercise control in their lives.

The magnitude of what Nipsey stood for and what he was able to accomplish through his music can liberate nations!

There's a reason why he was called Neighborhood Nip. He didn't get rich and try to leave his community behind, he saw the beauty in the area he was raised in and knew that with the proper investment his community can thrive despite the cards being stacked.

Nipsey was unapologetically a product of his environment but in the same breathe, he aimed to transform the very environment that raised him into an environment that could raise it's future better than it's past.

For those who grew up in the inner-city and didn't have guidance, music played a large role in raising what could be considered a lost tribe. Nipsey credits the likes of Scarface, Jay-Z, and Tupac for helping shape him into a man. He stated that without a male role model around he used lyrics to become a solid individual. The lyrics provided principles that you could live by. Nipsey provided the same. And what he did above all was show his neighborhood both near and far that you don't have to be ashamed of where you come from, nor do you have to transform into someone else to live your best life. You can literally build and live the life that you want by being authentically you.

In essence, Nipsey is so important because he is a direct representation of what is possible when you know your power. When you have an unwavering faith in yourself and full control of your life economically, you can create the rules as you see fit. You don't have to conform to a norm or switch up who you really are in order to achieve massive success.

2

The Making of Nipsey Hussle and The Ghetto Economic Trap

Nipsey Hussle was a proud member of The Rollin 60's Neighborhood Crips, which is a street organization based in Los Angeles, California. According to Wikipedia, The Rollin 60's was originally formed in Los Angeles in 1976 from the Westside Crips and has since spread to other cities in the United States. Membership is estimated to be between 6,000 to 8,000 people, making it one of the largest street organizations in the Los Angeles area. In many instances, when living in the inner-city, joining a street organization is a necessity and not something done by choice. The conditions in which the inner-cities have been forced into require a structure and code in order for its residents to survive. These conditions can be dated all the way back to the beginning of the formation of America and have always existed for the economic benefit of one group; the wealthy.

Racism is and has always been an economic and political strategy. Those who historically had wealth and power knew that the power of the people will **ALWAYS** be stronger than the people in power IF the people knew their power. This is why for centuries (and even today) wealthy people in power did (and do) their best to divide in order to conquer. They strategically make us focus on our differences instead of our similarities in order to make us choose a side that is conducive to their continual reign of power and wealth.

The book, *American Slavery, American Freedom* by historian Edmund Morgan does a great job of proving this fact. What starts out as a history lesson on conflicts between the British, Spanish, French and English; turns into an understanding of why the mass genocide of Native Americans and the enslavement of Black and White people occurred.

Motivated by an intense rivalry between England and Spain, the English wanted to "free" the Indians who were being oppressed by ruthless Spanish conquistadores. To the English, freedom meant something different and they thought that by colonizing North America, the Indians would be appreciative and submissive since they were no longer under Spanish rule.

As explained by Mr. Morgan, English-style freedom was naive, arrogant, and ethnocentric; which means evaluating other peoples and cultures according to the standards of one's own culture. This arrogance and ethnocentrism infuriated the English settlers and explains why they killed Indian men, women, and children and destroyed their cornfields, even though the settlers needed the corn to survive.

This level of hatred towards the Indians for their lack of appreciation of their freedom (that wasn't really freedom since they were still being colonized and controlled) is what the English settlers would use as the reason to begin racist practices that benefited the rich minority.

As tobacco became the major product that bought in riches for American planters, they needed to ramp up production to meet the demand. Planters would literally and figuratively work their laborers to death and as the need for more laborers to work new land became vital (land that was stolen once the old land was plagued with weeds), the desperation for a new workforce grew.

The conditions of the laborers got worse and worse which led to many of them complaining that they were being bought and sold like slaves. In 1622 Powhatan Indians attacked English settlements, which made it clear that the English and Indians would not peacefully coexist in the conditions in which the English place the Indians.

As the tobacco trade began to become a global commodity the class divide between the rich and poor started to become obvious. Because there was a shortage of white women, many wealthy widows held the power in creating the class separation. They were very particular about who they would marry, so the rich stayed rich and the poor stayed poor. Many young single and poor white laborers who were also male servants had a very slim chance of marrying up hence solidifying their economic and social status.

This is where things begin to take a turn. As the English settlers began to fix their labor issues with slaves from Africa, the conditions that both white laborers and black slaves faced we're almost identical.

Mr. Morgan explains that before 1660, white servants and black slaves suffered similar oppressive working conditions and began to form a unified front. They ate and slept together, they attempted to run away together and even began to have sexual relations together. In reality, there wasn't a real difference between how the wealthy treated enslaved Africans and how they treated the white working poor. The poor were the majority and if they continued to work together they could've eventually turned the tides, which was dangerous for those in power.

This is not to say that there weren't racist prejudices that existed, but before 1660 it was difficult to distinguish the difference between racial prejudice and class prejudice.

This lack of distinction threatened to shake the foundations of the new world that the English settlers were creating.

"The answer to the problem, obvious if unspoken and only gradually recognized, was racism," Mr. Morgan states, "to separate dangerous free whites from dangerous slave blacks by a screen of racial contempt."

Because racial hatred towards the Indians already existed, the English settlers did not have a hard time separating and creating content for enslaved Africans and the children of interracial unions.

To accomplish this, the settlers were able to get the government to create legal codes that were disguised as a way to protect their slave property and prevent rebellion, but also to reduce the confusion about what was possible for whites and what was possible for blacks. Giving poor whites hope and a leg up made them feel superior to blacks even though they currently suffered the same.

Racism became a tool that was used to achieve political and economic gain. In essence, racism allowed white men across the class divide to perceive a common identity which in turn allowed the wealthy to maintain control.

Fast forward to post-slavery and even post-civil-war, we will see this same type of government-sanctioned legal codes that were meant to divide and maintain control but also steal and maintain wealth.

According to the Treasury Department, between 1865 and 1874 newly freed slaves saved more than $57 million in the Freedman's Bank, which was a bank founded by President Abraham Lincoln after emancipation to help newly freed slaves and African-American soldiers integrate into the nation's economy at the end of the Civil War. The bank was headquartered in Washington, D.C. and had branches in 37 cities across 17 states, with the majority of the branches located in the south. It is said that over 480,000 African-Americans and institutions used the bank's services including OG abolitionist Frederick Douglass (who briefly served as its president). Frederick Douglass himself invested $10,000 of his own money into the bank which would equal $20 million in today's economy. A series of risky investments caused the bank to go into debt, but it was the decision to build a new building in Washington, D.C. that ultimately took the bank under. It is reported that their deposits were taken to build the new building in D.C., and they were never reimbursed. Many scholars believe that the Freedman's Bank's failure and the theft of all of their savings led to a distrust of all banking institutions for several generations among the black community.

There were attempts to hold those responsible for the thievery accountable but nothing ever occurred. Specifically, a Congressional investigation called for the indictment of several individuals but that was ignored. Congress even established a program to reimburse depositors up to 62% of their savings, but many depositors never received a dime.

At this point, racism was profitable on so many levels and as you will see by the continued legal and most times overlooked economic injustices, the creation of ghettos and the condition in which we find them in are no mistake. It is also important to note that despite it all, black people continue to thrive and overcome time after time after time.

Case in point: The Great Migration which occurred between 1916 and 1970, was a time where the economy started to boom in other parts of the country; especially the north. It is said that prior to the great migration 90% of Blacks lived in the south. Because of this economic boom, more than 6 million blacks left the South in search of a better life. However, what isn't talked about is that most blacks were fleeing due to acts of domestic terrorism such as lynching and other forms of disparaging brutality at the hands of the KKK, law enforcement, and racist white Americans. During this restart, many blacks had to abandon millions of acres of some of the most lucrative land in the U.S. which ultimately fell in the hand of their oppressors... "Still I Rise" (Maya Angelou voice)

After the migration tapered, legal segregation, government policies, and racism created what we call ghettos. These factors made it nearly impossible for blacks to live in any other neighborhood. The great migration was a result of white laborers in the north starting to create unions to force better working conditions. Similar to what the American planters did during slavery, wealthy business owners wanted to find a free or cheaper way to gain labor.

Enter the Blacks! To combat against paying laborers who were part of the unions, factory owners started to proactively recruit black male laborers from the south. Because white supremacy was at full swing by this time, factory owners knew that by hiring Black men they didn't have to worry about blacks and whites getting together to demand higher wages. Racism not only made the factory owners more wealthy but it also made sure that the power of the people would never materialize. The white laborers saw the migration of blacks as a direct threat to their livelihood. So, as a result, we begin to see racial violence in neighborhoods and at work. White supremacists were under the impression that simply touching a black body would lead to disease so they defended their neighborhoods by all means. If Blacks wanted to live in peace, they had to make a decision to live in worse neighborhoods and also work for less money than their white counterparts for doing the same job.

To add insult to injury, the government intervened to create racist policies that would ensure color lines were not crossed. Some examples of these policies included the provision that allowed homeowners to ensure that their property would never be sold to anyone other than whites for a certain period of time. This was literally written into their property deeds. Even though the supreme court found these policies illegal, many local cities and states continued to practice these provisions with no repercussions.

Ok, no big deal... They don't want us in their Neighborhoods so we'll build our own, said the Black trailblazers from Tulsa Oklahoma who created Black Wall Street, which was known as the wealthiest black community in America. Black Wall Street was said to have had 600 businesses, 21 churches, 21 Restaurants, 30 grocery stores, 2 movie theaters, 6 private airplanes, plus a hospital, a bank, a post office, schools, libraries, law offices, and even a bus system. This was all destroyed during the Tulsa Race Riot (or the Greenwood Massacre) of 1921, when mobs of white people attacked black residents and businesses in Black Wall Street. It has been called "the single worst incident of racial violence in American history.

So where were the cops you ask? According to many eye witness accounts, law enforcement supported the attacks against the Black Wall Street residents. It is said that law enforcement officials had refused to stop the organized white mobs and even encouraged white residents to throw flamethrowers at the black residents. It is also reported that the local Tulsa chapter of the National Guard had begun sending aircrafts over Black Wall Street and used this advantage to rain bullets on the homes of black residents.

This wasn't just an isolated incident; the deliberate effort to keep blacks as an underclass wasn't a conspiracy theory but in fact a well-documented pursuit. We can turn to federally backed home loans that strategically kept Black families out of the wealth-building process as exhibit A.

Starting in the 1930s and for the next few decades, the government underwrote home loans that essentially created what we know as the suburbs and essentially made many American households into homeowners. These loans though were not distributed fairly and in essence pushed white homeownership while blacks had to live in the inner-cities.

The Federal Home Owners Loan Corporation (FHOLC) was created as part of President Roosevelt's New Deal to distribute loans, and part of the process was to create maps that assessed the risk and reward of said loans.

One of the key components in assessing the risk of home loans was race. Both the race of the applicant and the racial composition of the neighborhood were taken into consideration. Black neighborhoods were coded red in these maps and denied home loans because black homeowners were deemed to be too risky a bet to take for government-guaranteed funds. This practice is what we know as redlining.

For decades to come, many other government loan programs use the same reasoning, then it trickled over to private lending and insurance companies also followed suit. As written into policy, being black was officially a financial risk.

What these policies essentially did was make it nearly impossible for black families to leave the inner-cities or build any wealth. It also made it very easy for white families to become homeowners and begin to build generational wealth through homeownership. Even whites who weren't racist benefited from these policies. It made great financial sense for them to take advantage of this new social restructuring.

At the same time, while these government-sanctioned racial policies were being enforced, the banks were making it easier for people to become homeowners. This is because prior to the New Deal, home loans had a shorter term of 10 years or less which meant higher mortgage payments and excluded many working-class families from being able to afford to buy a home. With the introduction of the 30-year mortgage, that also came with a small down payment, homeownership became a reality for many Americans... Specifically white Americans.

This was a significant time as it relates to the wealth gap because prior to this working class white Americans did not have a clear path to wealth accumulation but now they did. Their homes became an asset that they could pass down from generation to generation.

This is why I said earlier that blacks were forced into ghettos. It wasn't hyperbole, meaning I was not exaggerating for effect there were laws in place that created the inner cities.

I know that was a long history lesson but it is important to know if we truly want to understand why what Nipsey Hussle was doing was so imperative towards the fight for economic equality. But let's sum it up...

So far you have stolen labor utilized through a system called slavery, that turned into domestic terrorism during Reconstruction and Jim Crow laws that stripped wealth from formerly enslaved people, then an economic boom for all people in America occurs, but laws were put into place to exclude the people who actually built the country. Because of violence and unfair wage practices, the jobs that these people can get were not sufficient enough to help them live decent lives. Stuck, frustrated, and persecuted by the government and law enforcement; rebellion starts to ensue and we are introduced to the urban uprising.

This was a period of riots in the inner-cities against the establishment. It forced many in the inner-city to only trust themselves and those within their communities. This birthed the Black Freedom Movement as explained by Stanford University was the series of black protests that began with the Montgomery bus boycott of 1955-56 it became the most significant social movement of the 20th century.

The history books and many prominent national black organizations mainly stressed civil rights goals but most of the local institutions were seeking economic and political reform. The Black Freedom movement was characterized by unconventional and increasingly militant tactics, locally initiated protest activity, decentralized control, and an increasing sense of racial consciousness among participants. This birthed the Black Panther party and their ten-point program, and eventually birthed the Crips , which by some accounts was started by Stanley ("Tookie") Williams and Raymond Washington, both high schoolers in Los Angeles. Reports state that the Crips were founded in 1971 for protection from gang violence. Others claim that Washington, inspired by the Black Panthers, formed a political group in 1969 that evolved into the Crips.

Either way, there's no denying the rivalry that existed in the streets that led to bloodshed, death, and incarceration. Add the introduction of crack cocaine into the mix then you have a dangerous combination that devastated an already fragile African-American community. The introduction of crack caused the increase of addiction, deaths and drug-related crimes.

I can easily start talking about the CIA involvement in cocaine trafficking and how the drugs even got into Black neighborhoods. As well as the fact that at the same time drugs were being placed in the ghettos to fund a war overseas, the United States declared war on drugs here on our turf. Again, all of this may sound conspiratorial but according to Wikipedia, a 1986 investigation by a sub-committee of the Senate Foreign Relations Committee, found that "the Contra drug links included", among other connections, "[...] payments to drug traffickers by the U.S. State Department of funds authorized by the Congress for humanitarian assistance to the Contras, in some cases after the traffickers had been indicted by federal law enforcement agencies on drug charges, in others while traffickers were under active investigation by these same agencies."

This draws a clear connection. I could also talk about how this war on drugs (drugs that seemed to be placed in the ghettos by the very entities that are fighting against it) created this narrative about African-Americans that ultimately led to mass incarceration and how that became a tool for slavery by another name thanks to the 13th amendment.

The ghetto is a trap... literally. And Nipsey would learn this early, while still a young adult. As a proud member of the Rollin 60' Crips, Nipsey was very transparent about his role in the gang life. From violence to drug dealing, it was very apparent that Nipsey really lived that life. Nipsey's mother was African-American with roots that traced back to Louisiana, while his father was from a small country in eastern Africa called Eritrea. When Nipsey was 19 he took some of the money he earned from hustling and bought a plane ticket to his father's homeland. This trip would change Nipsey's whole perspective and the trajectory of his life forever.

Before the trip, He was just a young man from Los Angeles who was knee-deep into the gang culture with the hopes of beating the trap by becoming a rapper. After the trip, he became a Grammy award-nominated musician, music executive, an activist, serial entrepreneur, marketing expert, and real estate investor, who was committed to changing his community for the better

Nipsey stayed in Eritrea for three months and while he was there, he made some very meaningful connections but most importantly he was able to, for the first time in his life, see a place where the people who were in charge where all melanated and looked like him.

Ralph Waldo Emerson once said, "The mind, once stretched by a new idea, can never return to its original dimensions." That's exactly what happened to Nipsey. Once he got back to L.A., his mind was open to the possibilities of how things could be. At one point South L.A. in the Crenshaw District was his whole world... Now the world seemed bigger.

In a 2010 Complex magazine interview, Nipsey said, "If you don't know your full-throttled history, the whole story of how you came to where you are, it's kind of hard to put things together. [Going to Eritrea] filled in a blank spot for me, as far as understanding myself."

Let's analyze this, his trip to Eritrea motivated him in ways that really nothing else could because it instilled a sense of pride and reconnection to his roots.

This is an element of our culture that we have lost, at no fault of our own it was certainly strategically done, however, in Nipsey's death we must acknowledge that it is time to relearn who we really are and recognize our genetic divinity. Later you will see that Nipsey's mom encouraged us to "go back to our roots and find our creator and spiritual power," she was simply referring to our true culture and the spirituality of Africa not to be confused with religion.

African spirituality simply acknowledges that african beliefs and practices touch on and inform every facet of human life. For example, sickness in the indigenous African worldview is not only an imbalance of the body, but also an imbalance in your social life, which can be linked to a breakdown in family relations and most importantly your relationship with the ancestors. Having a greater understanding of the power your connection to your ancestors, the earth and universal law is empowering and deeply embedded in African culture. I encourage you to learn more through researching the foundations of African religions such as Yoruba, Cuban Santeria, Brazilian Candomble and Haitian Vodou.

With this new knowledge of self, tapping into his roots, and the idea that a community can be run by its residence, (similar to many communities in Eritrea) Nipsey decided to create a long-term strategy that we now know as "The Marathon".

This strategy would be run with his brother, friends, family, and strategic partners. In the next two chapters, we will dive deep into Nipsey's strategy and give you a guide on how you can use it to run your own marathon.

3

The Philosophy of Ermias Asghedom

Ermias Asghedom better known as Nipsey Hussle was fatally shot and killed in front of his Marathon Clothing Store on March 31, 2019. He was 33 years old. To many, his age of death may not have any significance but if you are into spirituality and/or numerology then you may understand why this matters. Spirituality and Numerology are difficult to explain. If you are in tune then you know it's power but sometimes things can seem far fetched. Even Nipsey's mother caught some backlash because of her tribute to Nipsey during his funeral. Questions began to swirl online, asking whether his mom predicted his death. Some even stated that she apotheosized her son, which means to elevate to, or as if to, the rank of a god; idolize.

As a husband, brother, father, and uncle I know for certain that a woman's intuition is real. But as a son I know that a mother's intuition is one of the strongest powers in the universe. As Nipsey's mom, Angelique Smith spoke to the crowd during Nipsey's memorial, she revealed that she had a feeling that something bad was going to happen weeks before her son was killed. She stated, "I had not slept for two weeks leading up to this event on Sunday (March 31), When I went there I was not at perfect peace." Once she got to the store, she knew that this was what she had been feeling. "My spirit said 'Oh, that's it.'" She continued to explain how she was now at peace and used this time to encourage his fans and the world.

"I have perfect peace," she said at the memorial. "I am happy. I am complete. I am strong. And if I can feel this way, you can, too."

She called Nipsey's father, Dawit Asghedom, to come stand with her on stage and continued.

"We call on the energies who guide and protect us as we make our way in life," she said. "We call on our ancestors to join us at this service. I would ask that all of our ancestors guide and protect us."

She also encouraged the audience to try and clean up their own lives.

"I want to encourage you to choose a vegan lifestyle," she said. "I want to encourage you to let [go of] your use of alcoholic beverages and narcotic substances. I want to tell you that we come from royalty and regality. I want to tell you that we are very loving and kind and a spiritual race of people. I want to tell you that we are very traumatized and pressurized people."

The strength that Nipsey's mom showed was a testament to her faith and spirituality. She wore all white which is considered a spiritual wardrobe in many African faith communities and is said to attract divine entities.

"Tap into your spirituality," Smith told reporters after the memorial service. "[My church] teaches African spiritual science and that's where I get my strength from. And as Black people, I want to encourage you to go back to your roots and find your creator and spiritual power."

This spiritual power leads me back to why the number 33 is significant. First, If you look into the meaning of Nipsey's name "Ermias" then you will come to find out that it means "Sent by God" or "God will rise." And as someone who doesn't believe in coincidences the fact that he died at 33 signifies that he was sent by God to deliver a message.

In Numerology, the number 33 is considered a Master Number, which means that it resonates at a higher vibration than other numbers. According to many numerology websites, when your angels send you messages containing angel number 33 expect your power to manifest and create will be heightened.

It is also said that Master Number 33 is generally called the number of the Master Teacher, and resonates at a highly spiritual vibration. The teachings that you receive from this Master Teacher will help you realize and achieve your higher purpose in life.

33 isn't the only Master Number. Master number 11 represents vision, Master number 22 combines this vision with action but Master number 33 offers guidance to the world.

The number 33 is not only significant in numerology but in the bible as well. According to BibleStudy.org, The number 33 is connected to a promise or the promises of God. The 33rd time Noah's name is used in Scripture is when God makes a special covenant or promise with him. The Eternal promises to not destroy the entire world again with a flood and seals His pledge with the sign of the rainbow (Genesis 9:12 - 16).

The 33rd time Abraham's name is used in the Bible is when Isaac, the child of promise, is born to him when he was ninety-nine years old (Genesis 21:1 - 2).

The significance of thirty-three is also seen at Jesus' death at the age of 33. It is said that his sacrifice, made in 30 A.D., was the fulfillment of countless prophecies and promises concerning the Savior of man. It is yet to be seen if Nipsey's work will save mankind but his teachings can surely help uplift families, communities, and disrupt a narrative and system of oppression. And in the words of Nipsey the Great... "All my life, been grindin' all my life

Sacrificed, hustled paid the price... Want a slice, got to roll the dice!!!

Without any further ado, the following 33 Ermiasism's will help guide you on your journey toward true economic freedom:

Er-mias-ism
/'Ur-me-ˈizəm/
noun
noun: **Ermiasism**

1. the philosophy of Ermias Asghedom aka Nipsey Hussle.
    - Derived from Nipsey's first name "Ermias" meaning "Sent by God" plus "Ism" which is

ism
/ˈizəm/
a distinctive practice, system, or philosophy,
typically a political ideology or an artistic
movement.

Ermiasism #1 - Find Your Purpose or You're Wasting Air!

"Define who you are and what you are, and be clear on that. Meditate on that and then, live and die by that."

-Nipsey Hussle

If you want true control over your life, then it starts with understanding your "why!" Why are you here and what is it you're supposed to be? Nipsey knew that everyone is placed on this earth for a reason. We all have a purpose and our goal in life is to find that purpose and give ourselves completely to it.

Many times people are so focused on what can give them the most amount of money or the most attention, that they miss out on doing being what they are absolutely passionate about. Life is lived fully when you allow yourself to be, not do! If you are busy doing then you will not have time to be who you really are. Nipsey was passionate about music, business ownership, prosperity, his community, his family, his well -being, and that of those he cared about. That was who he was in his being, not something he was doing. The distinction between being vs. doing is important as you find your passion.

Nipsey knew that his journey wasn't going to be easy but by staying true to his passion he was able to fulfill his destiny. His passion allowed him to be himself. People loved him, they related to him, and they felt him through his vibrations. When you walk into your being then you are aligned with your purpose and when you are aligned, the things you can accomplish are infinite. As Neighborhood Nip said in *Victory Lap*, "Find your purpose or you wastin' air."

Ermiasism #2 – Have Unwavering Belief In YOURSELF!!!!

"The most important thing, number one, is you gotta get rid of doubt. If you got doubt in what you're doing, it's not gonna work."

-Nipsey Hussle

To accomplish everything you want to accomplish in life you must understand that you were born abundant and anything you put your mind and grind to can be manifested in real life if you have an unwavering belief in yourself. No matter what, you have to move forward like failure is not an option...

In fact, failure isn't an option if you never give up. Failure is only possible for those who are not committed to themselves and their vision. Despite many setbacks, despite how many times he was told no, and despite the obstacles that stood in his way, Nipsey had so much belief in himself that he knew he would be successful.

In the famous "Our Greatest Fear" poem by Marrianne Willaimson, that says "Our deepest fear is not that we are inadequate. Our deepest fear is that we are powerful beyond measure. It is our light, not our darkness that most frightens us;" That's how Nipsey felt.

He never thought that he wasn't able to accomplish a dream, he just thought that he didn't dream big enough. When asked what advice he would give to a younger Nipsey Hussle, it would be... "Be more fearless!" He stated that all of his radical ideas is what has defined him. "That don't be my downfall, my downfall will be not going crazy, not having a higher expectation. Anytime I done set my sight on something that seemed way outlandish, it always comes back exactly how I seen it. So, I think I would tell myself [to] just put way bigger goals on the wall. Just have a bigger vision, have a higher expectation."

This is why you must have "unwavering belief!" Not belief that only accepts what is possible or probable but belief that allows you to go after your wildest dreams. If you believe it, then it can and will come to fruition.

Ermiasism # 3- Visualize and Plan For Your Dream (Know What it Really Takes... Don't Just Wing It)

"Thought is powerful in all phases. Even in my career, even in my life, things end up exactly how I visualized them."

-Nipsey Hussle

If you fail to plan, then you plan to fail, but how can you plan for something that you can't see? Visualization is one of the best-kept secrets of accomplishing your dreams and aspirations. In the song That's How I knew, Nipsey is heard rapping, "I seen it, I thought it, I dreamed it, I said it, I did it, I meant it, I taste it, I loved it, I need it, I want it, more of it, I fiend it, I'm godly, I'm gutter, I'm genius." These prolific words that double as an affirmation displays the level of foresight one must have in order to attract and maintain their true desires. But it can't just be random thoughts and wishes, they must be intentional based on what you truly want to accomplish.

Before Nipsey ever hustled anything else, music was the first dream. As a youngster, Nipsey knew that he wanted to be a rap star but in order to do so, he needed the tools and equipment. In visualizing and planning out his dream, Nipsey and his childhood friend Jermaine would pretend that they were building a studio in the backyard, clearing the dirt, sweeping and visualizing what their studio would look like. Once they really started to put a plan on paper and figure out how much money they would need to build their studio, it was then Nipsey started to put his manifestation to work.

Without a clear vision of what it will take to achieve your dreams, it will be nearly impossible to make them happen. How it happens should be left open to the universe but make sure you know what needs to happen then visualize on it to set your dream in motion. Faith without works is dead, so you must still be working towards your dream, but it starts with the vision.

> *"Before rap, my last name was my lifestyle, and when I visualize success it looked like right now."*
>
> *-Nipsey Hussle*

Ermiasism # 4 - Put Your Vision on Paper and Be Specific (Always Raise Your Bar)

"If you've got a plan, it's not just like a pipe dream. You have a step-by-step list of things to do to get to your goal."

- Nipsey Hussle

There is power in writing things down. Not only does writing your vision on paper help give you a roadmap and guide you on where you want to go but spiritually it signifies to the universe that you are committed to making your goal happen. Also writing your vision or plan down gives you a measuring stick to let you know how far you came. If you are just living life every day with no definite goals, then it will be hard to measure your success. On Nipsey's last breakfast club interview, Nipsey was asked about a lyric he mentioned in his Slauson Boy 2 mixtape. He talked about reaching his goal only to have to rearrange the list. Without that list, the vision would've been lost and the opportunity to raise the bar wouldn't have been present. Make sure as you are planning and working on your success, you continue to take it a step further as you achieve each goal. Life is a journey, not a destination.

"I have a clear cut vision on where I want to go"

-Nipsey Hussle

Ermiasism #5 - Study Those You Can Relate To

"I know how to get it out the trunk. [When it comes to the pioneers], I can relate to their origins, I felt like that's what happened to me. Everybody who came out of the streets into the independent grind and graduated that into being commercially successful, I could trace their steps."

-Nipsey Hussle

In my best-selling book, "Mind Right, Money Right, 10 Laws of Financial Freedom," I discuss a process called "See More, Be More," that essentially says that what a person can achieve is based on their expectations of themselves. How people perceive themselves and how far they go, has a direct correlation. If someone was born impoverished with limited experiences, the chances are that their expectations of themselves will be limited as well. Relatively, if someone has been exposed to more things, whether rich or poor, their expectation of themselves is now based on a broader range of exposure and life experiences, giving them a better chance at success.

This is exactly what happened to Nipsey. His success was a direct result of studying the independent music pioneers that came before him. Whether it's Percy Miller aka Master P with No Limit Records, J-Prince with Rap-a-lot, Bryan "Birdman" Williams and Ronald "Slim" Williams with Cash Money Records, E40 with Sick Wid It Records, or Jay-Z, Dame Dash, and Biggs with their Rocafella movement; Nipsey could relate especially because all of the people just named had their start in the streets and were able to successfully transition to become music moguls and make millions.

The blueprint that these pioneers set, coupled with Nipsey's unwavering belief in himself is what gave him the vision and audacity to even think that his goal was possible, let alone probable.

As you journey towards your success, make sure that you are identifying those people who came before you that you can relate to and model their success. Everyone is their own unique being, so you have to be the secret sauce, but it is a fact that success leaves clues. As you walk into your greatness, just the mere thought that your dream can become a reality will give you the needed boost, when the going gets tough.

> *"We the No Limit of the West, n****. Percy Miller at his best, n****. Jigga with the Rollie and the vest, n****."*
>
> *-Nipsey Hussle*

Ermiasism # 6 - Don't Let Lack of Money or Resources Stop You From Getting Started Towards Your Dream

> *"My thing is that I don't give no person that much power over my path that I'm walking. Not one person can make or break what I'm doing, except me or God."*
>
> *-Nipsey Hussle*

There's a famous saying that says, "It takes money to make money," and while that may be the case in some instances, that cannot be the reason why you don't pursue your dreams. When Nipsey Hussle started, he couldn't afford an engineer, so out of necessity, Nipsey learned how to record himself. This skill would help him perfect his sound going forward but also gave him the power and control necessary not to need anybody to fulfill his goal. He always kept his destiny in his own hands, and while he was very vocal on the importance of having a strong team, he didn't let the lack of resources be his obstacle.

Whatever your goal is, there is something you can do today that will move you closer to fulfilling your pursuit. Doing nothing because you lack money or resources just means that you do not want it bad enough. Start now with what you have.

> *"You've got to have faith in what you're doing and not take no for an answer."*
>
> *-Nipsey Hussle*

Ermiasism # 7 - Start Small, Think Big (Prove the Concept)

"I think you can give a pure artistic product if you understand how to build your own industry."

-Nipsey Hussle

One of the biggest misconceptions that most people have is that when you're a boss or own your own business, you work for yourself. The truth is, when you are a boss or own your own business, you work for the people. Without your target market, Fanbase, supporters, customers, consumers... Whatever you call them, without them, you do not have a business; you have a hobby.

It is crucial that as you establish your business foundation, as mentioned earlier, you begin to prove the concept. When Nipsey started his music career, he started hustling mixtapes out of his trunk and to people in his neighborhood. This was his real market research; will someone pay him for his music? As he continued to build a buzz but most importantly build bank, it was an indication that his music was worth something. If you want to see what people value pay attention to where they spend their money. Be intentional about selling your product or service to see how it is being received in the marketplace.

"Be truthful with yourself and other people, and try your best to make decisions outside of your ego."

-Nipsey Hussle

Ermiasism # 8 - Live In Day Tight Compartments

"Instead of trying to build a brick wall, lay a brick every day. Eventually, you'll look up, and you'll have a brick wall."

-Nipsey Hussle

Anyone who has ever tried to start something new knows that there are ups and downs with any venture. In Nipsey's case not only did he have to endure the normal turbulence that comes with starting a new venture but with the added pressure of his environment and the need to survive, it made his journey that much harder.

Nipsey always had big dreams and aspirations but he also knew that in order to reach those dreams and aspirations he needed to live in day-tight compartments. This means that he kept his overall vision in his mind's eye but also knew that the only real currency that he had was the present moment. Every step of the way, he wanted to stay focused on what he was working on at the moment to make sure it was the best that it could be. Instead of scattering his energy, he did one thing at a time to the best of his ability.

As you focus on your enterprise it is imperative that you know and plan the bigger picture, but instead of giving 20% to five things, you should give 100% to one thing, then move to the next. Once that one thing is operating efficiently, you can delegate what work is needed to maintain it while you work on the next. This is how dynasties are built!

"Whatever you do, homie, give your heart to it/ And stay strong."

-Nipsey Hussle

Ermiasism # 9 - Be Authentically and Unapologetically YOU!

"And it's possible to monetize your art without compromising the integrity of it for commerce."

-Nipsey Hussle

One of the things that Nipsey prided himself on was that he was 100% himself. His goal in life was to inspire those who came from similar backgrounds, specifically those who found themselves in gang life. Because of this, he was not shy to claim his affiliation with the rolling 60 Crips. He once said "As gang members, as young dudes in the streets, especially in L.A., we're the effect of a situation. We didn't wake up and create our own mindstate and our environment; we adapted our survival instincts."

This is why he was on a mission to do what he could to reach the people in a positive way. His mission to be authentic and to give people who he was, is what led to his massive success. In many interviews Nipsey recalls labels being afraid to do business with him because of past experiences with gang members or street figures who transitioned to music. Despite that Nipsey was clear that he didn't want to alienate his brand for business. Whenever you compromise for the sake of a dollar, the connection to your product or service will be short-lived.

Nipsey and his music will live for eternity because of his authenticity. When you throw on his music, his authenticity can be felt through your speakers. That can only happen when you're being unapologetically you. Out of the 8 billion people that live on this earth, you are the only YOU! Appreciate that fact and use that in your favor.

Never be afraid of who you are or what people will say about you because those who mind don't matter, and those who matter don't mind... (s/o to Dr. Suess)

> *"Life is about distinguishing yourself; it's about expressing the unique qualities of what you are and who you are and actually being loud with it."*
>
> *-Nipsey Hussle*

Ermiasism # 10 - Differentiate Yourself (Don't Blend In)

"It's a violation to blend in! When you stay in your lane, there is no traffic in your life."

-Nipsey Hussle

The biggest disrespect you can ever pay yourself is to try to be like everyone else but in the age of social media where you can literally become whatever you say you are sometimes it is imperative that you make it clear that you are different. Nipsey was not afraid to let people know that he was different. On his lead single for Victory Lap called rap N****s, Nipsey dedicated the whole song to explain that he wasn't like everybody else.

Some may look at this from the wrong perspective and feel like it is a little self-centered or arrogant but the truth of the matter is that if you're like everyone else then why would someone want to do business with you?

As you will see in the next chapter when we put our action plan together, one of the questions that is asked of you is, what is your unique factor? Make sure that you are keeping your receipts. Anyone can claim to be whatever they want to be, which in the spiritual realm is a good thing because as you speak it, you begin to manifest what you have spoken but... Make sure that as you are moving forward that you can back up what you're saying in real life. As Nipsey said, "Don't discredit the sacrifices that it takes to succeed. You can't just plop yourself in the ranks with n****s, that really put in work."

There's a big difference between "faking it til you make it" and "faith'ing it til you make it" One is for likes and for show and the other is with true intentions to manifest. Regardless of what spectrum you fit into, never let your true accomplishments fall under the radar. Talk your s**t and let potential partners or customers know your true value.

> *"We ain't equal because we both make a dope record, we ain't peers because we got a record deal or we in the rap game. Let's just be honest and let's deal with each other in reality. Just because you went to the studio and figured out the beat and got a cool cadence, don't necessarily mean I agree with the songs you make. I agree with you because of how you are living, how you are moving, this is just what I believe."*
>
> *-Nipsey Hussle*

Ermiasism #11 - Watch Your Surroundings

*"The company you keep has a large influence on the situations you bring to yourself. So, whatever direction m*****f*****s are heading in, whether it's rap music, production, or a 9-5 life, whatever it is; you gotta surround yourself with people that's likeminded and focused on the same goal you're focused on. Birds of a feather flock together."*

-Nipsey Hussle

They often say that you are the average of the five people you spend the most time with. If you want to see your future, just pay attention to your surroundings.

Nipsey knew that in order for him to take his life and career to the next level, he needed to connect with like minds. And not just for the sake of connecting with people but Nipsey was into making genuine connections. From Jay-Z, to Kendrick Lamar, Puff Daddy, YG, and the list goes on. He was even revered by many athletes like LeBron James and Stephen Curry. But it wasn't only the people at the top, he also surrounded himself with love; with the fans who appreciated his music. No one was ever too small for him to connect with.

Watching your surroundings isn't about economic or social status but about mindset. Are the people you around building or destroying. Are they adding value to your life or are they taking it away? Make sure that you are constantly networking and making genuine connections. At times it may seem like a tedious process but as the saying goes iron sharpens iron.

"Circle got smaller everybody can't go"

-Nipsey Hussle

ERMIASISM # 12- BUILD A SOLID TEAM

"if you put a camera on the team you'll see that what's going on is not regular; we are different. Yes, I get most of the credit because I'm the face, but it's my team who helps keep it together."

-Nipsey Hussle

Nipsey has always been willing to give credit where credit is due. Because he is the name and face of the brand, most people automatically attribute all of the success to him. Nipsey will be the first to tell you that the success of the brand is a team effort.

Nipsey has always dedicated his life to the hustle and so as someone who appreciates and cherishes hard work, he understands that in order to succeed he needs people on his team who are equally as dedicated as him. When speaking on his team he says, "My team is different, if you put a camera on the team you'll see that what's going on is not regular. The homies sitting around, smoking weed and catching the groupies is not the type of team we got."

Make sure as you are assembling your team, that you are putting together a cohesive group of people who are in the business of winning. As the saying goes, "Make sure everybody in your "boat" is rowing and not drilling holes when you're not looking."

*"'Bout to make my partners look like f****n' geniuses, We was in the Regal, it was me and Steven, We done took a dream and turned it to a zenith."*

-Nipsey Hussle

Ermiasism # 13 - Define What Success Means to You!

> *"Success to me is just being able to do what you love to do and support yourself all through."*
>
> -*Nipsey Hussle*

To some people success is making $1million dollars, driving a foreign car, and living in a mansion. For others, success is simply waking up and being the best that they can be. Two completely different sides of the coin, but nonetheless these are both marks of success.

What most people get wrong about success is that it isn't determined by society, it isn't determined by your family, and isn't determined by your material possessions. It is solely determined by YOU. Nipsey knew that regardless of what people thought about him, it was really what he thought about himself that matter the most. He lived his life with pure intentions and understood that he was going to define what success looks like for him.

There were many opportunities that Nipsey could've taken advantage of, that to the outside world would've been "success" but it didn't align with his definition, so he had to stay true to himself.

Case in point, with great respect, admiration, and relationship with Rick Ross, Nipsey had the opportunity to sign to MMG. There is no doubt about it, that the Hip-Hop world would've been in a frenzy had this materialized. But as Nipsey explained, he made a promise to his team to fully execute the plan that they had set forth and to go against that would not have been the right move to make. Ultimately, Nipsey stuck to his guns and it worked out exactly how he envisioned.

Make sure that whatever you say success is, that's what you aim towards. Do not allow the noise of the outside world to tell you what success looks like for you. This is your journey, your race, your marathon, so success should always be on your terms!

> *"They say every man is defined by his reaction to any given situation/ Well who would you want to define you?/ Someone else or yourself?"*
>
> *-Nipsey Hussle*

Ermiasism # 14 - Trust the Process

"You learn all the secrets to the game on your way up. Most folks want to skip the process when you skip steps, you miss the lessons."

-Nipsey Hussle

When you have unwavering faith that something will happen, it doesn't mean that it will happen easily. In fact, most things that happen easily, do not last long because long-term success has struggle built into it. It isn't struggling just for the sake of struggling but it is struggle that helps build your character, your skills, and gives you the wherewithal to keep going when the going gets tough.

Nipsey knew this first hand. From his studio being raided by police to having to hustle when music didn't seem like it was working out to getting arrested right after he signed his first record deal, to getting dropped or agreeing to separate from that record deal because it wasn't working out, to being harassed in his neighborhood by law enforcement, and the list goes on. Despite all of the ups and downs, Nipsey trusted the process and wasn't shy about sharing the game. Nipsey once said in an interview with Big Boy, "I'm not gonna lie and portray this ultimate poise like I've been had it figured out, no, I just didn't quit! That's the only distinguishing quality from me and probably whoever else going through this or went through this or is gonna go through this, is that I didn't quit. I went through every emotion with trying to pursue what I'm doing and I think that's what gonna separate whoever's trying to go for something."

Please understand that struggle is part of the journey! What you go through on your way to success is as important as the success itself! NEVER for one second take your struggles for granted! Embrace them, Love them, and Use them to get you the life you deserve! As the saying goes... "You have to fight through some bad days to earn the best days of your life."

Ermiasism # 15 - Stick to the Script But Be Flexible

> *"We got turned down, we failed, had setbacks, had to start over a lot of times. But we kept going at it. In anybody's case, that's always the distinguishing factor."*
>
> *-Nipsey Hussle*

From day one Nipsey was after ownership and freedom. He came into the game with a clear vision to be an independent artist. His goal was simply to sell 50,000 units of his music and be able to tour and make at least $15,000 a show. He watched Master P and studied the successes of the Jay-Z's and Jay Prince's that came before him and thought to himself that he could do the same.

Well, this was his initial plan but life would have a different direction for him to take. Nipsey winds up signing a record deal with Epic Records and he explains that when he did the deal he was on the run from the law. He didn't have a warrant out for his arrest but one of his friends had just got arrested for something he was involved in. He knew it was just a matter of time.

He thought that was going to do a lot of jail time, so he had to reconfigure his original plan. Signing to Epic was Nipsey's way of trying to get a big infusion of cash, so he would be able to fight his case since hiring a lawyer would be expensive. After celebrating the signing of his deal, he did indeed get arrested but ultimately he just ended up doing probation.

This is a testament to what will inevitably happen in most

journeys. You will have a plan but circumstances may alter that plan just a bit, but regardless of what happens you must stick to the script and be flexible.

Just because he signed a deal out of necessity didn't mean that the vision of independence was lost. He decided to go a different route but because he always kept his true intentions in his mind, he wind up still getting what he wanted. Eventually, the deal with Epic didn't work and in time he was able to buy back his music which put him back on the path of true independence just like he wanted. As Nipsey said, "Sometimes you have to take two steps back to take ten forward."

Always remember that even though you have a plan for your life, there can always be circumstances that derail those plans. In the same breath, it is important that you don't give permanent energy to temporary things. Adjust to those temporary setbacks and keep pushing towards your destination.

> *"You gotta go hard, you gotta believe in yourself. You gotta have a sense of humor to know that the bulls**t is gonna happen, you can't be too serious about it or too emotional and fake when it does. You gotta just stick to the script, believe and have overwhelming confidence. Be your own biggest fan, your own biggest believer, and put it on your back and carry the weight."*
>
> -Nipsey Hussle

Ermiasism # 16 - Own Your Now and Future

> *"The new mindset is we don't want advances, we want equity. We don't want 1-off endorsements, we want ownership."*
>
> *-Nipsey Hussle*

In the words of the Honorable Shawn Carter, until you own your own you cannot be free. Our whole human existence is about living our purpose, loving our life and having the freedom to live on our terms. But as the saying goes, freedom isn't free. In order to live in a world where basic necessities cost money, your freedom is in essence attached to your income or wealth.

Nipsey knew that in order to live life on his terms he needed to be an owner. He wasn't just an artist; he was also a music executive that understood the nuances of running a business. He also understood the power of the hip-hop culture and knew that by delaying gratification in the form of not taking an advance or signing to a label (opposed to partnering with them) would be a slower grind to build wealth, but more lucrative in the long run. When you look at all of the money he made from streaming because he owned his masters, the wait was more than worth it.

A lot of times we exchange ownership for instant gratification, whether it's selling our time for money, or giving up equity in our business to raise capital, or signing a contract that gives away our intellectual property. If you are in it for the long term and want true liberation, then you must own you're now and future.

There may be a lot of bumpy roads along the way but when

you reach the top of the mountain you'll be glad that you kept your ownership. If you believe in yourself, and your product or service, and know that what you are putting out has value, then eventually you will get all that you deserve.

> *"I own my company. I own the asset of this whole industry which is your masters, your intellectual property, you know what I'm saying, your publishing. So, you know, your metrics and what you gauge [as] an achievement is actually a peon, underboss way of looking at it. Because, you know like, I'm not in it for the fame. Everybody wanna be seen and held at the highest regard obviously but, you know, you can't cash that out, you can't take that to the bank."*
>
> *-Nipsey Hussle*

Ermiasism #17 - Be Creative on How You Monetize Your Brand (Build an Eco-System around your main product or service)

> *"We're creating an ecosystem, from production to consumption. Not only do we own the supply chain, but we can curate the experience. From the ownership of the actual master to the retail experience and marketing the product, to consuming it. That's the same model as Apple."*
>
> *-Nipsey Hussle*

I can literally write a whole book on supply chains, vertical integrations, and eco-systems, but for the purpose of this book, you must understand that building an eco-system was what accelerated Nipsey's wealth and rise to stardom.

Owning the supply chain means that you are fully responsible for your product or service from production to consumption. Case in point; the fact that Jay Z owns Tidal and uses his own streaming service to release his music means that he cut the middleman out completely. He owns the whole process from production to consumption. Before I continue I want to break down what an eco-system is Please see below:

ec·o·sys·tem

/ˈēkōˌsistəm/

noun

Ecology

plural noun: **ecosystems**

1. (in general use) a complex network or interconnected system.

Owning the whole eco-system means that you have total control over anything that is connected to your product or service. For instance, as a music artist, whose main product or service is releasing new music, merchandise and touring live concerts is part of that ecosystem. These products and services become a source of income that derives directly from the music that the artist puts out.

This is why there is such a movement against 360 deals. In essence, a 360 deal is someone else owning your eco-system. The true definition of a 360 deal is a business relationship between an artist and a music company. The company agrees to provide financial and other support for the artist a.k.a. an advance as well as support in marketing, promotion, touring and other areas... In layman's terms, the company gets a piece of everything.

As Nipsey and his team started to realize how influential their marketing tactics were, they decided to start a marketing company. They also decided to create an experience by opening up their own store called Marathon Clothing where people could physically experience Nipsey's music or buy merchandise; there was also an online component. One thing people didn't know about Marathon Clothing is that it's known as a "smartstore.'

According to Wikipedia, a smartstore is a brick-and-mortar retail establishment using smart technologies like smart shelves, smart carts, or smart cards and usually delivers their services via the Web, smartphone apps, and augmented reality applications in real stores.

The Marathon Clothing Store allowed customers to purchase merchandise and use an app to preview exclusive content from Nipsey. This is another example of Nipsey owning his eco-system.

Owning his eco-system is what allowed him to understand his customers better. With the data he received from the people who shopped with him online and at his store, he was able to start his "Proud to Pay" campaign in 2013. This is where he infamously charged $100 for fans to purchase a physical copy of his mixtape Crenshaw.

According to a rap radar interview, Jay Z was so intrigued by the idea that he bought 100 copies. This bold and audacious idea allowed him to make $100,000 off of something that he was offering for free and in turn, gave him the capital necessary to fund his next project.

Nipsey understood that customers buy at different price points; so the same customer who was on YouTube or Datpiff looking for a free mixtape was probably not the same customer that would buy his product for $100. You only know this if you own every aspect of your business.

When he said "I integrated vertically y'all n****s blew it," he wasn't bragging or exaggerating. He was letting it be known that other artists have the power to own their destinies but instead, they keep signing record deals.

Don't get me wrong, there are going to be instances when it makes sense to outsource or delegate a part of your business to another company but that's where strategic partnerships come into play. When you create a strategic partnership, as we will talk about next, you still are a part of the ecosystem and in turn maintain control of your destiny.

Ermiasism # 18 - Build Strategic Partnerships

> *"We should all think outside the box right now, and we should all be aware that we're empowered and we're* gonna do radical s**t right now!"
>
> *-Nipsey Hussle*

There is no question about it that Nipsey is a man of integrity and one of the things that intrigued me the most about him was the fact that he knew what he wanted but would never take more than he deserved.

He revealed during a Breakfast Club interview that he was trying to sign a deal with Atlantic records for close to three years, but it never materialized because he wasn't fully ready. Nipsey and his team had specific terms that they were looking for in a strategic partnership and at the time that they were requesting these terms, Atlantic did not feel that Nipsey was at the point where he can demand those terms.

Nipsey agreed and instead of looking for a different partner, he and his team decided to get to work to increase his worth so that the deal can make sense.

One of the reasons why Nipsey wanted a strategic partnership with Atlantic was because Atlantic is one of the largest record labels in the business today. A relationship with them would give Nipsey access to opportunities and resources that purely independent artists couldn't do by themselves.

Due to the structure of the deal, Nipsey was not able to reveal exactly what the deal entailed but he did say that this deal was aligned with some of the other joint ventures that have been done in the past.

The other important aspect of this strategic partnership was the actual team behind the company. Nipsey knew that it was important to know who he was going into business with. No matter what the reputation of a company is, it is only as good as the people who run it. The executives from Atlantic had many years of experience in the music business but also had a reputation for helping independent artists create joint ventures.

As you decide whether your business requires a strategic partner to take you to the next level, understand that any partner that you approach must see value in what you are offering. This should go without saying but this works vice-versa as well. Do not enter into a partnership with anyone or entity if there isn't a mutual benefit. The best deals are made when it is a win-win situation.

Successful Independent artists create a movement for their music, they build their brand, they expand their fan base and once that is done they create the leverage to be able to ask for specific terms within any business deal. This is true for you, and whatever business you're in.

Once you can increase your value in the marketplace whether it's by revenue or purely the size of your movement a.k.a. how many eyeballs do you influence, it becomes easier for companies to see your worth and more likely that they will be willing to write a check. If you want to succeed in anything increase your value and everything else will fall into place.

"I know that if you go hard and your product is solid you got the advantage."

-Nipsey Hussle

Ermiasism # 19 - Know Your Numbers (Streaming advantage)

> *"We was getting rap money. So it was all progress. That was amazing to me that we can get paid off music. And it kept growing. Slowly, it was just growing. So it was like shit I'm cool. As long as it keep making progress. I ain't on nobody else timetable."*
>
> *-Nipsey Hussle*

Men lie women lie numbers don't! In order to solidify your success, it is imperative that you know your numbers. Know what it cost for you to produce your product or service, know how much you are selling this product or service for, understand what are the profits made from your product or service, and surely understand what your break-even point is; which is the amount of money you need to make in order to recoup for expenses. Once you hit break-even, everything after that becomes a profit.

Nipsey began to see the benefits of owning his masters, when he started to look at his streaming numbers. At one point iTunes sales were his largest revenue generator but as streaming got more popular and as he continued to build his brand, he started to see a shift in his streaming numbers.

The great thing about streaming is that it is a gift that keeps on giving. In the finance world, we call this residual income or passive income, because you record your music one time and you're able to get paid from it over and over and over again.

This was a similar case with CDs and records. The difference was that you owned the CD or record and so once you bought it, you always had it (unless you lost or damaged it). Music and even movie streaming have allowed companies to keep getting paid for the same content. You are never an owner but constantly leasing.

Understanding this concept fits in well with knowing your numbers because whatever product or service you are providing it is also imperative that you understand what business model makes the most sense for you to pursue. It is impossible to get somewhere if you don't know where you want to go. Knowing your numbers the best way to measure which direction your company is going.

Ermiasism #20 - Use the System, Don't Let the System Use You

The Spook Who Sat by the Door is a book that came out in 1969, written by Sam Greenlee. It is the fictional story of Dan Freeman, the first black CIA officer, and of the CIA's history of training persons and political groups who later used their specialized training in gathering intelligence, political subversion, and guerrilla warfare against the CIA.

In the song Blue Laces 2 Nipsey raps, "I'm 'The Spook By The Door' this the infiltration," and while some may have understood what he meant, this deserves some further explanation.

While it is now obvious through his action that Nipsey's goal was to uplift his community, he had to study and learn the system in order to do so. He stated, "In terms of hip-hop, the power structure has a prescribed persona that they expect to act a certain way, but I used they intention against them."

What he meant is that as a known member of the Rolling 60s Crips, many within the music business would assume that the music Nipsey would make, would perpetuate gang violence and continue to tear down the urban community.

And while there may not be a conspiracy to hold the black community down, I hope that the earlier chapter explained why lack of knowledge of self would be beneficial to the bigger power structure.

Instead of Nipsey allowing himself to be used as a weapon against his own people, he put the medicine in the candy. He was able to infiltrate and gain the eyes, ears, and hearts of many people that would normally be missed by the message of financial empowerment and community revitalization. In fact, after his death, there was a decrease in gang violence and many of the rival gangs decided to call a truce in Nipsey's honor.

In many ways, there are systems that are set up to perpetuate the marginalization of certain groups, but if you understand the systems, you can also infiltrate it to your advantage. Think about how Uber understood the taxi system, realized that there were weaknesses and loopholes that existed, then created a multi-billion dollar business addressing that issue.

As you continue to journey towards your business dominance always find ways to use any obstacle as a springboard for your success.

> *"I took my wildest dreams then mapped them out. I go for mine like it's overtime, me and my niggas had to struggle so we over shine."*
>
> *-Nipsey Hussle*

Ermiasism # 21 - Know Your Power and Take What You Deserve

"It's cliché to say, work hard, don't quit. I would really say find yourself and find what's your why, what's the motivating force behind you? And build around that."

-Nipsey Hussle

Often times when I say "Nipsey's community" it could be understood to mean Los Angeles or the Crenshaw District, but in fact, Nipsey represented all of us. He was a mouthpiece and community activist for the hoods in America, in Eretria, and anywhere that the system was designed against a marginalized group.

Nipsey represented them and inspired them all. One of the biggest things that these groups have in common is that they have the power but only if they knew it. In the song Dedication, Nipsey says, "I want real n***a reparations," and what he's asking for is access.

Many of the billion-dollar industries that black and brown people have helped build, do not give those same people a seat at the table. Whether it's technology, film, television, finance, or cryptocurrency as an example, black and brown people are underrepresented to an alarming degree. This inequality could and would stop if black and brown people knew their worth and used it as leverage.

The reason why the Montgomery bus boycott was so effective was because Black people decided to exercise their power, which directly affected the bus company's bottom line.

There are many instances where the middleman, who gets the lion share of the profits does the smallest amount of work. Knowing your worth and taking what you deserve is about understanding this dynamic and finding ways to collectively not settle for less. The African proverb says, "if you want to go fast you go alone, if you want to go far you go together," knowing your power means that you understand cooperative economics and know that the power of the people will always be greater than the people in power.

Ermiasism # 22- Keep All Your Money In (No Money Out)

> *"I'm about seeing long-term, seeing a vision, understanding nothing really worthwhile happens overnight, and just sticking to your script long enough to make something real happen."*
>
> *-Nipsey Hussle*

Nipsey Hussle's record label is named "All Money In," and the significance of this name whether intentional or not; was that because Nipsey what adamant about ownership, focused on vertical integration and supply chain, and also owned his ecosystem, he literally kept all money in.

Then when you think about the fact that he still lived and worked in his community, he made his presence known in the community, started businesses in the community, bought property in the community and eventually invested in the revitalization of the community, then you know that "All Money In, No Money Out was more than just a name that represented a company.

What Nipsey was doing was changing the economic fabric of his community for generations to come. According to Maggie Anderson, author of "Our Black Year" "The lifespan of a dollar in the Asian community is 28 days, 19 days in the Jewish community, and approximately six hours in the African-American community! Some may be shocked by those numbers but instead of pointing the finger, Nipsey decided to do something about that.

As it relates to you and your financial freedom; It is imperative that you make sure you are using your money to support the communities that you care for. Keeping all money in that community assures that programs get funded, that businesses continue to flourish, the youth of your community get to see entrepreneurship firsthand, and if residents continue to buy back the block, those very youth can have a choice in which direction they want to take their lives.

Keeping "all money in, no money out" is also a strategy used by many small businesses to decrease their tax liability. When you become a business owner, the money that you pay taxes on, are the funds that are left over after expenses. A simple formula says revenue or income minus expenses equals net profit a.k.a. the money that you have to report for tax purposes. Many wealthy people know that as you lower your expenses, you lower your tax obligation. With this in mind, they create a LLC or Corporation and intertwine their daily expenses within that corporation.

This allows money that they would've been spending anyway, as an individual with no tax benefits, to serve as a tax write off or deduction of tax obligation within a corporation. This is totally legal and is used every day by wealthy people to keep their tax obligations low, which we now recognize as "all money in and no money out. Please speak to your accountant or CPA before you implement the strategy.

Ermiasism # 23 - Create MailBox Money

"Yo you can look up and that's when at the highest level of business, That's they model, equity! At the highest level of business, there's mailbox money."

-Nipsey Hussle

Nipsey was no doubt a business mogul who created multiple streams of income to secure his financial freedom. What comes with these streams of income is what he calls mailbox money. Mailbox Money is like what it sounds like; Money that just unexpectedly comes in the mailbox. In this technological age, it also statements at the end of the month, or direct deposits straight to your bank account, either way, Nipsey was operating from the highest level of business and used the strategy that creates lasting wealth.

It's one thing to have assets and wait for them to appreciate over time but it's another thing to have these assets pay you income while appreciating overtime. An example is if you own your home; that's an asset that will most likely appreciate over time but if you live in it, it isn't giving you an income. But if you own property and you rent out this property, the asset (the property) will increase over time but while it's doing so, you are also receiving income each month a.k.a. mailbox money.

This was evident in the fact that Nipsey wind up owning the property that houses his store, but not only just the store but all of the other adjacent properties as well, meaning that he would receive mailbox money from the other tenants of those businesses.

In order to build wealth, you must change your relationship with money. Nipsey knew that he couldn't look at money as something he had to work for; instead, money was something that had to work for him.

Remove yourself as the employee of money and become the employer. By creating passive income, you remove the dependency on physical labor and free up more time for you to live stress-free, doing what we want to do.

Making money work for you aka Mailbox Money, is an essential part of financial freedom. As long as you continue to keep your "work for money" mentality you will never be in control of your finances or your life. When the economy is doing badly and jobs are being cut, those who work for money are the ones who are affected the most. This is also true for business owners who work for money.

The people who have money work for them may be affected as well but on levels so small that it doesn't disrupt their day to day lifestyle. Creating passive income is the only way to alleviate the stress that comes with economic downturns.

Ermiasism # 24 - Protect Your Most Important Assets

"Million Dollar Life Insurance on My Flesh."

-Nipsey Hussle

Nipsey often rapped about trust funds, life insurance, and other estate planning tools. He knew that if he really cared for his family and wanted them to reap the benefit of his hard work that there were things that needed to be set up to make them whole in the event of an untimely demise.

And this wasn't just talk either... Shortly after Nipsey's death, many celebrities came to the aid of Nipsey's family by setting up a goFundme page and encouraging their followers to donate money towards the family, especially the kids. This kind gesture was respectfully turned down by the family because Nipsey really had life insurance on his flesh and trust accounts where he deposited racks.

When most people hear the words "will," "trust" or "estate planning" they automatically think that these are things reserved for millionaires and billionaires. This couldn't be the furthest thing from the truth; regardless of how much money you have, you must have a plan for what will happen to your assets and who should receive the things you own after you leave this earth.

An estate plan can be something as simple as having life insurance for your family and naming a beneficiary for your retirement accounts, or as complicated as having several trusts for different purposes in addition to your will.

Regardless of what direction you decide to go, it is important that you put a transition plan in place to maintain the continuity of your family business that outlives you. Estate planning is more than just having a will. It is a plan that is put in place in order to lessen the financial impact of your death on those you leave behind.

At a minimum, estate planning is for the benefit and care of your loved ones, making the legal and financial issues easier to deal with if you pass away. But it is also a tool to transfer wealth and maintain your family legacy. Every competent adult should have a succession plan aka an estate plan especially if you have children.

"Open trust accounts deposit racks."

-Nipsey Hussle

Ermiasism # 25 - Take Calculated Risk to Grow Your Wealth

"Keep my eye on this game and let the money invest."

-Nipsey Hussle

No one has ever achieved anything great by playing it safe. In life, it takes taking risk to be wealthy. Nipsey showed us first hand that he was willing to invest in himself. From selling everything that he owned to invest in his music equipment to being willing to jump into unchartered waters to make his dream come true.

That investment in yourself may not always pay off immediately but rest assured if you never give up it will pay you tenfold. The goal though is not to take stupid risk but to take calculated risks. This means that you do your due diligence before you jump into anything but nonetheless you should take risk if you want to see your wealth grow.

Below are five things to look out for when investing:

1. Any investment or deal that promises big returns in a short amount of time or seems too good to be true.

2. Anyone who can not verify their credentials and prove they are a legitimate business.

3. Any person or company that uses peer pressure as a way to entice you to invest.

4. Anyone who tries to do you favors or uses their charm as a way to make you feel obligated to invest.

5. Anyone who makes the investment or deal seem like a limited time offer or a once in a lifetime opportunity.

*"F**k livin' basic, I'm takin' risks."*

-Nipsey Hussle

Ermiasism # 26 - Always Put Assets Over Liabilities

"I'd rather invest in real estate — invest in some assets as opposed to trick all my money in diamonds and cars — it look good but at the end of the day you're losing value. It ain't appreciating, it's depreciating. (I'm trying to get) a real asset. Take care of my people."

-Nipsey Hussle

From day one, Nipsey came into the game dropping jewels. In a 2006 Interview with legendary Hip-Hop Journalist Davey D at The Russell Simmon's Get Your Money Summit, when asked why he was not blinging, with jewelry and diamonds. He immediately gave us a lesson on the difference between an asset and a liability. To Davey D's surprise, the then up and coming rapper said "You know, all of that is cool and all, for the image but all them are liabilities. I rather invest my money in assets, like real estate that appreciates in value, opposed to tricking all my money on liabilities, like diamonds and cars that lose their value as soon as you drive them off the lot."

This priceless wisdom is why you should always put assets over liability. The more you grow your assets, the higher your net worth will be. And the higher your net worth, the more opportunities you have to create generational wealth. When Nipsey said, "It isn't cool to be in the club spending all of this money, or having cars and jewelry – but you don't own any real estate? a fourplex? If the answer is no, you're not a real hustler," He was saying that it's not OK to work hard for money just to throw it down the drain. Instead, if you had some assets, you can let those pay for the liabilities. That's the Hustler's way!

Make sure that you are always looking at ways to purchase assets a.k.a. things that you own that increase in value. If you want to buy things let your assets pay for them

"Never stop grindin', cherish no possession."

-Nipsey Hussle

Ermiasism # 27 - Always Keep Your Stash Full

"Got a safe that's full of Franklins."

-Nipsey Hussle

The goal of being financially free is necessary so that you can live the life on your terms but even if you have everything mapped out, you're doing everything right, and you have all the right things in place, situations can still pop up and take you in a different direction. When Nipsey bragged about having a safe for the Franklin's... Benjamin Franklin that is, he was saying that you should always have a stash.

This stash can serve as a cushion for unexpected expenses. It makes sense to have at least 6 to 8 months of expenses in an account liquid; meaning you have direct access to it.

It is possible to be asset rich but cash poor so make sure that even though it might pain you to watch this money just sit in the account, make sure it's accessible if need be.

Ermiasism # 28 - It's Ok to Splurge Responsibly

"Champagne While I Shop, Hope I Splurge Foolish, I close Escrow Twice This Month, Both Commercial Units".

-Nipsey Hussle

Nipsey admits that when he got his first seven figures he went on a mile splurge. Jewelry shopping, car shopping, and visiting some of the finer restaurants.

If you listen closely it may sound like a contradiction but the reality is that it is OK to splurge responsibly. This means that as you are setting up everything else in your financial household you should also set aside some money to spend.

Not allowing yourself to spend in proportion to what you have budgeted can lead to a relapse and the feeling of self-deprivation which can result in spending money foolishly.

As long as you are taking care of everything else within your financial wheelhouse a mild splurge and there won't shake your financial foundation. Just don't let the material things define you.

"Material things ain't nothing, you feel me? At the end of the day it's who you is."

-Nipsey Hussle

ERMIASISM # 29 - STAY AHEAD OF THE GAME (INNOVATE)

Nipsey was always a step ahead of the game and when he felt he wasn't, he picked up the books, attended the conferences, and found the people that can help increase his knowledge.

He believes that the time that we're living in is an incredible time. He said, "It's like a gold rush, it's never been a time like this in our generation." He is specifically speaking about tech and the close proximity to Silicon Valley. He continued, "It's our equivalent of the Gold Rush with everybody movin' to California. This technology has empowered everybody and it's as big as you wanna make it and, you know, it's as far as you take it."

His belief was that it is important to innovate and except what Technology is doing. If you fully embrace it, his prediction is that big companies are going to crumble, Giants are going to fall and new companies are going to pop out of nowhere and take over... He wanted to be part of that new wave. This is also why he was very involved in Blockchain and cryptocurrency.

If you look at history and go back as far as you want; the one thing that has ever been constant is change. No one would ever think that the Roman empire could fall but it did. As you are building your empire, do not get so stuck on how things are that you are not willing to learn and innovate when necessary.

"I just believe in ownership... I believe in investing in yourself... Your foundation should be strong."

-Nipsey Hussle

Ermiasism # 30 - Buy Back the Block

"Last time that I checked they was sellin' zones in the set, Make a quarter mill no sweat."

-Nipsey Hussle

Before we can discuss Buying Back the Block we first have to define and explain two words... Gentrification and Opportunity Zones.

Gentrification is a process of changing the character of a neighborhood through the influx of more affluent residents and businesses.

An Opportunity Zone is an economically-distressed community where new investments, under certain conditions, may be eligible for preferential tax treatment.

Often times Opportunity Zone incentives are used to Gentrify a neighborhood and is a common and controversial topic in politics and in urban planning.

In a freestyle that served as a tribute to Nipsey Hussle, Jay-Z eloquently explained what Nipsey was doing with the Opportunity Zones and why it was such a pivotal initiative. He said, "Gentrify your own hood before these people do it/ Claim eminent domain and have your people movin' /That's a small glimpse into what Nipsey was doing For anybody that's still confused as to what he was doing."

Eminent domain refers to the power of the government to take private property and convert it into public use. The Fifth Amendment provides that the government may only exercise this power if they provide just compensation to the property owners. In this case, Jay-Z was saying that Nipsey and his partners were using this opportunity zone legislature to gentrify Crenshaw before others came in to do it. This is the first time we see this being done on a grassroots level and "for the people" instead of trying to change the socio-economic structure of the neighborhood.

Jay-Z continues, "The neighborhood is designed to keep us trapped/ They red line us, so property declines if you live by blacks/ They depress the asset and take the property back/ It's a ruthless but a genius plan, in fact,/ So now we fighting over scraps." If you remember earlier when we discussed redlining, gentrification is such a controversial topic because it seems that after years of creating ghettos, gentrification aims to displace low-income residents who never had a choice, to begin with.

Nipsey decided that he would give the hood an opportunity to own and love where they live. Nipsey was also laying the blueprint for other celebrities, athletes, and influencers to teach them how to give back to their community and make money without having to displace those who really need it.

Opportunity Zones are one way you can start the process of buying back your block but there are many others. Make sure you are exploring different ways that you can be a blessing to others.

"I own the block where I used to hustle from 8 am to 10 pm. I hustled, then I rented now me and David Gross will own in Crenshaw."

-Nipsey Hussle

Ermiasism # 31 - Give Back to the Community

"At on point I wasn't proud of my lifestyle..Now I wake up knowing that I'm doing what I'm here to do."

-Nipsey Hussle

The law of giving and receiving is a dynamic universal law. In order to activate receiving you must be willing to give that which you are seeking. By being a good giver you are allowing the abundance that the universe has for you to circulate in your life. Nipsey was blessed, so it's no shock to hear that he was a big giver. The fact that he was selfless in thinking about the place that made him who he was, is a testament to his character, his integrity and to what matters to him most.

Nipsey wanted the residence of his community to have a different experience than the one he had growing up. He made sure that the basketball courts were paved for the children and also offered STEM education through his technology and Coworking center Vector 90. This venture was also a way to make sure that the youth in his community found jobs and they had an opportunity to thrive. We spoke about ecosystems earlier and even though this wasn't about music, Nipsey wanted to create an ecosystem around tech.

In describing Vector 90, Nipsey said, "So, basically, [there are] these different office spaces rented by entrepreneurs that are starting apps, or got skincare companies or product lines. So, they got investors in the building with David Gross, who's the founder and my partner, and in myself... every year we're gonna be able to do a first round of seeding for one of the entrepreneurs. They can make a pitch and say, 'This is what I'm doing. This is what we need to take it to the next level,' and they can have access to investments in the same building," He also said, "Instead of having to fly somewhere. It's right here in the Crenshaw district."

The great thing about the type of giving that Nipsey and his partners were involved in is that it was a type of giving that wasn't purely philanthropic but instead an entrepreneurial venture that gave back. This is called Social entrepreneurship which is an approach by start-up companies and entrepreneurs, in which they develop, fund and implement solutions to social, cultural, or environmental issues. A win-win for everyone involved.

Giving back to your community should be a part of your overall business strategy and should be done from a place of passion. You can also donate your time to many organizations who are in dire need of fresh blood to help build the next generation.

> *"I taught all my homies how to fish. Some caught more than others. Some said they rather be fed. Some passed me up in the process. But at the end of it all, I know I ain't hide the game from my people and I'm real for that."*
>
> *-Nipsey Hussle*

Ermiasism #32 - Build a legacy

"I'm more focused on giving solutions and inspiration more than anything."

-Nipsey Hussle

To many, death is a scary thing because no one really knows where you end up when life is over. And for those who have ever lost a loved one, it can be one of the toughest things you ever have to deal with because at the moment it feels as if you have lost your loved one forever. The truth of the matter is that no one really dies if they made "the dash" matter when they were alive in the physical. The dash is what goes in between your date of birth and the day you transition.

Nipsey Hussle made sure his "dash" stood for something. It was his explicit intention to uplift a generation of people who did their best to play the hand they were dealt with.

Nipsey was a role model who showed us a new way to be successful. He showed us that no matter what your background is, or where you started, you can, at any moment, decide to change the trajectory of your life.

He also showed us that you can aim for maximum profit in all you do while simultaneously helping your community. You don't have to wait to make an impact on someone's life.

During an interview with ABC News, Nipsey's brother Samiel Asghdom aka Blacc Sam said, "Nipsey was somebody that believed in the process of hard work, determination and just the positivity of somebody staying in the area that he grew up in and making something out of nothing," Sam continued to reflect and labeled his brother as a role model to the community, to the kids, and to the mothers and grandmothers and the community that watched him grow up.

Nipsey was serious about his community. He had many initiatives he was a part of including "Destination Crenshaw" which is a 1.3 mile "open-air museum" of permanent and rotating art exhibitions that is planned for Crenshaw Boulevard along the light rail line which at the time this book was written is currently under construction.

According to Councilmember Marqueece Harris Dawson, It is meant to be a celebration of the largely African-American community in South LA and Nipsey Hussle had a significant role in birthing the project. Nipsey even inspired actress, writer, and producer, Issa Rae to buy property in LA.

Nipsey understood the importance of leaving a legacy and even though he was taken from us in the physical, his name will live FOREVER! When you think about your work and all that it is you are trying to BE in this world, make sure your work will have a lasting impact on the world at large.

> *"I call it 'dropping the rope'. You've got to drop a rope. Everybody got to climb up, but you gotta drop the rope."*
>
> *-Nipsey Hussle*

Ermiasism #33 - Run Your Race But Remember It's a Marathon.

"If you really think about the metaphor of the marathon, as in life, it's about endurance it's about preparedness, it's about mentally breaking through the barriers that tell you I can't keep going when you know you're more capable than you think you are or even conscious of."

-Nipsey Hussle

The marathon metaphor has been around for a while and the message has always been clear but Nipsey brought the point home and made it even clearer; if you run your race and keep going despite adversity then you will achieve all of your dreams and aspirations. We all have a purpose in our lives but in living that purpose we often focus on the destination that we believe our purpose will take us instead of the journey that it is meant to provide.

We know what we want and some of us want it to happen overnight and even though we know it doesn't work like that, we still have hopes of a smooth ride.

Nipsey understood that you couldn't cheat the grind. He knew that success was a mindset and a process. Despite how glamorous many online entrepreneurs make the grind look, he recognized that there are a lot of ups and downs and accepted the fact that in order to achieve long-term success, he was going to have to push past the pain of being uncomfortable. The grind came with long hours and many instances of near surrender but despite that, he knew that success was his as long as he never gave up.

Nipsey didn't focus on immediate wealth but instead on the type of wealth that never ended. In an interview, he stated, "We playing the long game. We don't want the money to stop when we go. When we can't work no more. We want it to outlive us, we want it to be generational." This is the mindset of a marathon winner, someone who has the big picture in mind and will make some short term sacrifices in order to ultimately win the war.

As you remember and celebrate Nipsey Hussle, never forget that his actions spoke as loud as his word. He wasn't just giving us a metaphoric theory that he heard or read in a book somewhere; he gave us his life, his experience, and a front-row seat to how to manifest your destiny. If I can paraphrase Nipsey the Great... All he was trying to do, was hustle and motivate... Choppers to throwaway, hustle the Hova way. That's why we followed him, we knew he knew the way!!!

Long live Nipsey Hussle! In the following chapter, you will be given a 12 step guide to running your own marathon. The Victory Lap Action Plan will take all of Nipsey's blueprint and give you a step-by-step guide to becoming a success.

> *"I'm about seeing long-term, seeing a vision, understanding nothing really worthwhile happens overnight, and just sticking to your script long enough to make something real happen."*
>
> *-Nipsey Hussle*

4

The Victory Lap Action Plan

"Success or greatness come with a roller-coaster ride... anybody can apply the marathon concept to what they do."

-Nipsey Hussle

When running any race, a Victory Lap is a celebratory extra lap of the race track taken after you have finished the race. As we run our own marathon, to solidify our Victory Lap or to assure that we finish as winners, the following is an Action plan broken down into 12 steps. These 12 steps represent each distance that needs to be taken in order to reach the end of the marathon. Remember, success is a process so make sure you don't try to skip any steps.

***200 meters:** 1/8 mile (1/2 time around a track)

Find Your Purpose

This first leg of the race is the foundation. Without it you are wasting air! Your "why" will keep you going!

***400 meters:** 1/4 mile (1 time around a track)

Speak Your Purpose into Existence

You need definiteness of purpose! Once you find your "why" you have to celebrate your victory every day before you've materialized it in real time. "I AM" are the two most powerful words in the universe. What goes after it will ultimately determine your life.

***800 meters:** 1/2 mile (2 times around a track)

Create a Business Plan for Your Vision

If you expect to be successful, you must have a specific plan on how this will happen. Your business plan will be your guide that dictates the actions you take to achieve your goals.

***1,500 meters:** .93 miles (3 3/4 times around a track)

Create a Marketing Plan for Your Vision

Once your business plan is together you must create action steps that will get the word out about your business. Your marketing plan will be your guide to how to build awareness around your business.

***5K (or 5,000 meters):** 3.1 miles

Build Your Team

Even if you have to start your business as a solopreneur, make sure you understand who else you need on your team to succeed. Whether these people are going to be your partners, full-time employees, or contractors, you MUST have criteria for the type of characteristics you are looking for in a team member.

***10K (or 10,000 meters):** 6.2 miles

Prove Your Concept

Now that you have the foundation of your business intact, it is time to prove your concept and get your first sale. Until you can get someone to pay you for your product or service you have a hobby, not a business.

***15K:** 9.3 miles

Create Your Eco-System

Now that you have proved your concept and have made your first sale, now it's time to create an Eco-System around your business to own your supply chain and create multiple streams of income.

***20K:** 12.4 miles

Strengthen Your Skills

It is imperative that you remain in the know about your business and the things that affect your business. You should read books and trade magazines, find a mentor or coach, take courses, join an accountability group or do all of the above. It is important that you stay a step ahead of the game.

***Half-marathon:** 13.1 miles

Build Your Stash

It Is vital to the longevity of your business and for the development of your financial freedom that you begin the process of creating a financial freedom fund that contains at least 6-8 months of expenses.

***25K:** 15.5 miles

Diversify Your Income

The average millionaire has 7 sources of income. If you are reliant on only one source of income you are committing economic suicide. Make sure that you are finding different ways to diversify your income and not put all of your eggs in one basket.

***30K:** 18.6 miles

Protect Your Assets

It is necessary to begin the process of protecting your assets. The work that you have put in to get to this place cannot be put in jeopardy. Make sure that you have insurance, a will, and an estate plan to protect your legacy and the people that you love.

***Marathon:** 26.2 miles

Become a Philanthropist (Give-Back)

There is a Universal law that says, "The more you give, the more you get." As you continue to build your legacy, never forget about where you come from and those who have supported you on your journey. Make sure you a giving back; whether it's time or monetary resources.

*200 METERS: 1/8 MILE (1/2 TIME AROUND A TRACK)

FIND YOUR PURPOSE

Questions to help you explore you find your purpose.

Instructions:

- Find a quiet, peaceful, place where you will not be disturbed.
- Answer each question below, think about it, and then write down what comes to mind without analyzing, editing, or judging.
- Most importantly, enjoy the moment and enjoy the process of self-discovery!

Questions:

I lose track of time when I am...

I feel great about myself when I'm...

If I knew I couldn't fail I would...

If money wasn't an issue I would love to spend my time...

My perfect day would consist of...

Three things I love about myself are...

I would regret not doing these things in my life...

If I knew I was going to die one year from today I would...

At my funeral I would like to hear... (what would each speaker say about you and your life; what kind of friend, family member, colleague were you; what character would you like them to have seen in you; what contributions and achievements would you want them to remember; what difference did you make in their lives; what is your legacy?)

These are the things I want to change about the world to make it better... (what issues in society or on the news make you most angry, what causes do you strongly believe in or connect with?)

Recall the happiest moments in your life. What were you doing? What were the circumstances? What is the underlying theme, if any?

Out of all of my accomplishments, both big and small, I am most proud of...

____

____

____

____

____

These are the people who inspire me most...

____

____

____

____

____

____

What gives you the most pleasure? What makes you smile? (activities, people, events, hobbies, projects, etc.)

____

____

____

____

____

____

What are you good at? What qualities do you have that you are really proud of?

____

____

____

____

____

____

What do people typically ask you for help in?

____

____

____

____

____

____

What were some challenges, difficulties, or hardships you've overcome? How did you do it?

____

____

____

____

If you could get a message across to a large group of people, who would those people be? What would your message be?

What are some common themes or things you notice in your responses?

What are things you discovered about yourself?

____

____

____

____

____

____

Review all of your answers. Take as much time as you need to think about each of your answers in depth. Ask yourself how you feel when you read your answers. Note which ones move you, and which ones make you feel alive. Now, write as many answers to the final question as you can until you feel moved, extreme joy, or are even brought to tears. Once you do this you will know your purpose. If you need more space to write, feel free to use a separate piece of paper.

My Life's purpose is...

1. ____

2. ____

3. ____

4. ____

5. ____

6. ______________________________
7. ______________________________
8. ______________________________
9. ______________________________
10. ______________________________

*400 METERS: 1/4 MILE (1 TIME AROUND A TRACK)

SPEAK YOUR PURPOSE INTO EXISTENCE

Below write down ALL of your deep desires in the affirmative using I AM. For example, if your desire is to be a millionaire then you will write I AM a Millionaire. Don't hold back and don't limit yourself. Now, add these affirmations as a daily calendar reminder on your smart phone and recite them every morning when you wake up and before you go to bed.

*800 METERS: 1/2 MILE (2 TIMES AROUND A TRACK)
CREATE A BUSINESS PLAN FOR YOUR VISION

EXECUTIVE SUMMARY *(Complete this section at the end of the planning process)*

What is the name of the business?

____

What are your business main goals and objectives?

Who is your target market? Who will purchase the majority of your products or services?

Is your business a sole proprietorship, partnership or corporation?

What is the total amount of financing required, and what will that money be used for?

Who will manage your business? What skills or experience do they offer?

What are some factors that will make you successful in the market place?

BUSINESS DESCRIPTION

Please summarize your business concept:

What type of business are you going to operate?

Manufacturing ☐ Retail ☐ Service ☐

What types of trends/growth patterns/challenges are occurring in your sector?

Form of business ownership:

Sole Proprietorship ☐ Partnership ☐ Corporation ☐

Why have you chosen this business opportunity?

1. ______________________________
2. ______________________________
3. ______________________________
4. ______________________________
5. ______________________________

Where is your business located?

____

Why was this location selected?

What major assets or equipment do you already have pertinent to the business operation?

Item	Value
______________________	$ __________
______________________	$ __________
______________________	$ __________
______________________	$ __________
______________________	$ __________
______________________	$ __________
TOTALS	$ __________

What will be the hours of operation?

____

Are there any necessary permits and licenses for your business? If so, what are they?

Who are the key people managing this business. How many employees will you have?

Complete a SWOT Analysis detailing your strengths and weaknesses, any opportunities you can take advantage of and any threats to your business and how you intend to deal with them.

THE PRODUCT OR SERVICE

Describe specifically what your business will do. What product or service will be provided?

Are there any unique features or benefits of your product or service? What is your competitive advantage?

If you manufacture a product, describe how it is made. If you retail a product, describe how you will source it. If you provide a service describe how you will provide it. (Attach additional sheets if necessary)

Describe your ability to meet the needs of your customer.

Are there any existing copyrights or patents?

What is your store/factory/ office/ mobile unit design and layout? (Attach floor plan/photos etc.)

What is your pre-start strategy to get your business ready to operate?

What are your technology requirements?

What geographic market will you cover or sell to?

What is the size of your demographic within your geographic target area?

Who are your competitors, and what are their strengths and weaknesses? Complete a SWOT analysis describing their strengths and weaknesses and how these are opportunities and threats for your business.

Who are your suppliers? Why have you chosen these suppliers?

What are your delivery costs? What is your turn around time?

What are the seasonal trends of your business? (Example: January-March=20% of sales; April-September=40% of sales; October-December=40% of sales).

What are your projected sales for year 1? year 2? Why do you think these projections are reasonable to expect?

How will you price your product? Will the market accept that price? Can you make an acceptable profit?

What are your competitors charging?

How will your product be distributed?

Is pick-up and delivery relevant to your operation?

What is your cost to obtain the product you sell? Use specific examples.

What is your markup percentage?

State any discounts, credit policies, or terms of payment.

What are your projected margins? Does this match up with you income statement?

What are the benchmarks for your industry? (Attach the benchmark report in your appendix) How does your business compare? What are the differences and why?

FINANCIAL ANALYSIS

START UP COSTS

Item	Dollar Amount
Equipment	
Building	
Land	
Vehicles	
Opening Inventory	
Marketing and Promotion	
Renovations	
Licenses and Permits	
Legal Fees	
Office Supplies	
Business License/Permits	
Other	
Total Start up Costs	
Minus Owners Investment	
Total Financing Required	

Do you require a loan for your business? How much? What will the loan be used for?

What are your projected sales for the first year? Second year?

Do you pay cash for goods and materials you sell, or are you billed on a 30 day basis?

How much capital (Cash or Assets) have you contributed towards the business?

Do you have enough positive cash-flow to operate if you do not meet your projected sales?

What are your options if you do not meet your sales projections?

When will the following be paid? What month?

Insurance Premium ______________________

Employee's Wages (e.g. weekly) ______________________

Business Taxes ______________________

Insurance ______________________

HST ______________________

Will you have any security deposits to make? (Example: electricity, telephone, PST, installation, first and last month's rent)

What is offered as security for a loan? (If Applicable)

Description	Value

What percentage of your customers will pay you in the same month that they purchased your product or service?______%

When will the remainder of your customers pay you? 30 Days ________% 60 Days ________%

What will your sales be for each month over the next year? (Start with your 1st month of operation)

Sales	
January	
February	
March	
April	
May	
June	
July	
August	
September	
October	
November	
December	

*1,500 METERS: .93 MILES
(3 3/4 TIMES AROUND A TRACK)
CREATE A MARKETING PLAN FOR YOUR VISION

MARKET ANALYSIS

Who is your target market and why are they potential customers? (Age, sex, education, income, marital status, work and needs).

Do you have any customers who have indicated they will or may buy from you? If not identify some potential customers who you intend to target:

What geographic market will you cover or sell to?

What is the size of your demographic within your geographic target area?

Who are your competitors, and what are their strengths and weaknesses? Complete a SWOT analysis describing their strengths and weaknesses and how these are opportunities and threats for your business.

MARKETING STRATEGY

How will you inform customers about your service or product? How will you promote your business? Complete a detailed outline of your strategy and marketing mediums. Why will this be effective? Include a cost analysis.(Attach additional sheets if necessary)

*5K (or 5,000 meters): 3.1 miles
Build Your Team

PERSONNEL

What will be the owner's specific duties?

What other employees will be required and for what purpose? Have you identified who you will hire? Is it difficult to find workers in your industry?

What is your pay scale? Remember to include MERCs (mandatory employment related costs) in your expenses.

Who will do the monthly bookkeeping?

Why are you qualified to successfully manage this business?

What are the job descriptions and responsibilities of the employees you plan to hire?

Who are the key advisors for your business? (Example - accountant, lawyer, mentor)

*10K (OR 10,000 METERS): 6.2 MILES

PROVE YOUR CONCEPT

Please plan to speak to at least 3 people per day about your product or service. Use the space below to track your progress: Remember you will miss 100% of the shots you don't take

*15K: 9.3 MILES

CREATE YOUR ECO-SYSTEM

What is your main product or service?

____

What Product can you create one time that is an extension of your main product or service that can be sold over and over? List 3-5:

1. ____
2. ____
3. ____
4. ____
5. ____

Is there an experience that you can create around your product or service that you can charge a monthly fee for? List them below:

____

____

____

____

____

____

____

Do you have the necessary skills to execute on the above? Are there any additional people you need to hire to execute these ideas? List your thoughts below:

*20K: 12.4 Miles
Strengthen Your Skills

It is imperative that you remain in the know about your business and the things that affect your business. Use this sheet to plan out your continued learning:

10 Books I will read this Year:

1. ______________________________
2. ______________________________
3. ______________________________
4. ______________________________
5. ______________________________
6. ______________________________
7. ______________________________
8. ______________________________
9. ______________________________
10. ______________________________

3 Trade Magazines I am going to subscribe to:

1. ______________________________
2. ______________________________
3. ______________________________

My mentor or Business coach is:

☐ ____________________

I will take these 3 online courses this year:

1. ____________________
2. ____________________
3. ____________________

My accountability group is:

☐ ____________________

*Half-marathon: 13.1 miles
Build Your Stash

FINANCIAL FREEDOM FUND WORKSHEET

To figure the amount that should be saved in your financial freedom fund (fff), fill out this worksheet.

Grocery bill for 1 month		x 6 months	=	$
Gas/oil, electric, and water for 1 month		x 6 months		$
Mortgage or rent for 1 month		x 6 months		$
Car payment or transportation for 1 month		x 6 months		$
Other mandatory debt payments for 1 month		x 6 months		$
Total amount I will need to keep in my financial freedom fund				$

*25K: 15.5 MILES

DIVERSIFY YOUR INCOME

Below are the Common Types of (Passive) Streams of Income. Below, jot down some ideas on creating an income from each category:

1. Interest – from a variety of loans, either to individuals (peer to peer lending or private notes) or companies (bonds, notes)

2. Dividends – from investments, partnerships

3. Capital gains – from the sale of investments

4. Royalties – from products you sell or license

5. Rental income – from real estate

6. Business income – From Franchising a business and letting someone else run it.

*30K: 18.6 MILES

PROTECT YOUR ASSETS

For this step please Make sure you get professional help from your financial advisor, an estate-planning specialist or a lawyer specializing in estates. The goal is to setup a will, trust, and life insurance, here's a list of steps that gives an overview of the estate planning process:

- [ ] Make a list of all your assets and liabilities.
- [ ] Purchase life insurance
- [ ] Start a family discussion about who should be the guardian for your children.
- [ ] Check and update your current beneficiaries on your IRA, 401(K)'s, LIfe Insurance policies, etc;
- [ ] Review the current estate tax exemption limits so you'll know how much you can transfer to heirs' tax free.
- [ ] Determine how your money will be distributed upon your death (family, charity, etc.).
- [ ] Discuss your funeral arrangements with your spouse or family.
- [ ] Seek the assistance of a certified estate-planning attorney.

Keep in mind that direct transfers to your spouse are not taxed - these assets are not taxed until s/he dies (this is called a marital deduction).

Below are some Estate-Reduction and Planning Options

- Use trusts to maximize the exclusion and avoid probate. Trusts help you do so because they are designated to a beneficiary.
- Take advantage of charitable donations to reduce your estate.
- Use your estate to pay family educational and medical expenses as these are tax deductible.
- Loan assets to family members to minimize your estate.
- Buy life insurance to help pay estate taxes, but remember life insurance will provide payouts only under certain conditions (executor or beneficiary should be owner).
- Utilize annual gifting to minimize taxes and maximize the value to your loved ones on your will.
- Set up durable powers of attorney.
- Establish your funeral and burial plans.

*Marathon: 26.2 miles

Become a Philanthropist (Give-Back)

Creating a giving plan for ______________ YEAR

ANNUAL GIVING PLAN
Funding areas Local Global Organization Amount Percentage Legacy wishes

CULTURAL ARTS

____

____

____

____

____

____

EDUCATION

____

____

____

____

____

____

SOCIAL PROGRAMS

ENVIRONMENT

ANIMALS

RELIGIOUS AFFILIATIONS

SUPPORT PROGRAMS

HEALTH-RELATED

BUSINESS DEVELOPMENT (MICRO)

____

____

____

____

____

____

SCIENTIFIC RESEARCH

____

____

____

____

____

____

TOTAL

5

The Nipsey Hussle Business School: Business Terms We All Should Know

Accounts receivable

This is the amount of money your customers or clients owe your business for goods or services you supply them. This total value can give you a snapshot of the amount owed to your business at any given time. Some banks will lend your business money based on your receivables.

Accounts payable

Accounts payable is a measure of how much you owe your creditors for goods or services supplied to you.

Angel Investors

An Angel Investor is normally a wealthy investor who was also a successful entrepreneur in the past. Their great knowledge and past experience allows them to not only give money to startups but also mentor entrepreneurs and give them advice, which can be even more valuable than the money itself.

Assets

"Assets" in its simplest form is anything that you own that increases in value. For business, its the cumulative financial holdings. These are usually classified as current or fixed. Current, or short-term, assets include cash or inventory. Fixed, or long-term assets, include equipment or land.

B2B/B2C

B2B or a business-to-business venture is when a business supplies goods or services to other businesses. On the flip side, B2C or a business-to-consumer venture is when a business supplies goods or services directly to an end-user or consumer.

Balance sheet

A Balance Sheet is a key financial document that provides a snapshot of business's assets, liabilities and owner's equity.

Bootstrapping

Bootstrapping is when an entrepreneur personally invests his or her own money into the startup without help from outside sources. When an entrepreneur bootstraps it shows they're fully invested in their startup and have complete faith in their business succeeding since failure could personally ruin them financially. This is called "sweat equity."

Business Strategy

A business strategy is a set of competitive moves and actions that a business uses to attract customers, compete successfully, strengthening performance, and achieve organizational goals.

It outlines how business should be carried out to reach the desired ends.

Business Model

A Business model is the "how" for the successful operation of a business, identifying revenue sources, customer base, products, and details of financing.

Capital

Wealth in the form of money or other assets owned by a person or organization or available or contributed for a particular purpose such as starting a company or investing.

Cash flow

Cash flow is the movement of money in and out of your business. You want there to be a higher flow of income into the business than there is an outflow of expenses from the business. This is called a positive cash flow.

Crowdfunding

Crowdfunding or crowdsourcing allows entrepreneurs the opportunity to present their business or idea to an entire community of potential investors who can then decided to invest funds in that entrepreneur's business or startup. Currently, the JOBS Act allows startup companies to raise up to $1 million in funding from crowdfunding sources.

Enterprise

Another name for a business or company.

Escrow

A bond, deed, amount of money or other document kept in the custody of a third party and taking effect only when a specified condition has been fulfilled.

Expenses

The money you spend to operate your business. This includes incurring expenditures for equipment, utilities or inventory. For those that are self-employed, legitimate business expenses are tax-deductible.

Fixed Asset Base

These are a business's bread and butter aka all the revenue-generating assets a business has, like facilities, machinery, vehicles, and equipment. These assets are what keeps the business running and are used to conduct the everyday operations of the business.

Infrastructure

Infrastructure refers to the basic facilities, structures and services upon which the rest of a business is built. It is common to think of infrastructure as physical things but basic software and services can also be considered infrastructure.

Joint Venture

When two or more parties start a new venture but each party retains their distinct identities.

Leverage

The ratio of a company's loan capital (debt) to the value of its common stock (equity). Also used borrowed capital for (an investment), expecting the profits made to be greater than the interest payable.

Liabilities

Liabilities are debts your business owes another person or entity. Like assets, you'll have to define liabilities as current or long-term. Current, or short-term, liabilities might include an expense payable to a supplier. Many business loans are long-term debts.

Meritocracy

Meritocracy is a system in which people are rewarded on the basis of talent, effort, and achievement, rather than factors such as heredity or wealth.

Net profit

Also known as your "bottom line." Net profit represents total revenues less total expenses. This figure is especially important at tax time. This is because you pay self-employment taxes as a percentage of net profit.

Net loss

If your total expenses exceed your overall revenues, you have a net loss. The risk of a net loss is one of many strong reasons to keep company costs under control.

Owner's equity

Owner's Equity refers to the owner's part of business assets usually represented as a percentage.

Paywall

(On a website) an arrangement whereby access is restricted to users who have paid to subscribe to the site.

Private Equity

Private equity is generally when private investors seek to support and add value to startup companies through long-term investments. Venture capital is a common source of private equity.

Profit margin

Your profit margin tells you how much profit you get to keep as it relates to your sales. There are three types of profit margins: gross, operating and net. Calculate these by dividing the profit (revenue minus costs) by the revenue.

Return on Investment (ROI)

Return on investment is a crucial term that all entrepreneurs need to be familiar with. Return on investment (ROI) lets business owners know whether or not they received a return from the money they invested into their business. To calculate the Return on Investment take the profit and divide it by the total amount of money that was invested into the company, and that equals the return on investment or ROI.

Revenue

Revenue refers to the income you get from your business activity.

Seed Capital

Seed capital is the money used starting out to fund a startup company. Seed capital can come from a variety of different sources such as crowdfunding, venture capital, business loans, personal loans, family and friends, and grants from business associations and the government.

Strategic Partnership

A strategic partnership is a relationship between two businesses or entities, usually formalized by one or more business contracts. A strategic partnership will usually fall short of a legal partnership entity, agency, or corporate affiliate relationship.

Supply Chain

The sequence of processes involved in the production and distribution of a product or service.

Terms

Clause or provision that constitutes a substantive part of a contract and may create a contractual obligation breach of which could be cause for legal action.

Vertical Integration

In microeconomics and management, vertical integration is an arrangement in which the supply chain of a company is owned by that company. Usually, each member of the supply chain produces a different product or service, and the products combine to satisfy a common need.

Working Capital

Working capital are any funds a business has that can be spent freely. To calculate the working capital a business has, take its current assets (short-term funds) minus current liabilities (short-term liabilities) and that equals your working capital. For example, if you had $10,000 in current assets and $5,000 in current liabilities, your working capital would be $5,000.

360 Deal

In the music industry, a 360 deal (from 360° deal) is a business relationship between an artist and a music industry company. The company agrees to provide financial and other support for the artist, including direct advances as well as support in marketing, promotion, touring and other areas. In laymen's terms, the company gets a piece of EVERYTHING!!!!!

6

The Nipsey Hussle Book Club

"I'm focusing on the music, but I still got a cold library of books that I've either read or I plan on getting to."

-Nipsey Hussle

Blood in My Eye by George L. Jackson

Blood In My Eye was completed only days before its author was killed. George Jackson died on August 21, 1971, at the hands of San Quentin prison guards during an alleged escape attempt. At eighteen, George Jackson was convicted of stealing seventy dollars from a gas station and was sentenced from one year to life. He was to spent the rest of his life -- eleven years-- in the California prison system, seven in solitary confinement. In prison he read widely and transformed himself into an activist and political theoretician who defined himself as a revolutionary.

Between the World and Me by Ta-Nehisi Coates

For Ta-Nehisi Coates, history has always been personal. At every stage of his life, he's sought in his explorations of history answers to the mysteries that surrounded him -- most urgently, why he, and other black people he knew, seemed to live in fear. What were they afraid of? Coates takes readers along on his journey through America's history of race and its contemporary resonances through a series of awakenings.

Decoded by Jay-Z

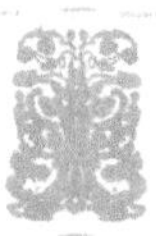

Decoded is a book like no other: a collection of lyrics and their meanings that together tell the story of a culture, an art form, a moment in history, and one of the most provocative and successful artists of our time.

Heal Thyself: For Health and Longevity by Queen Afua

The healer differs from the medical doctor in that the medical doctor is a learned and trained technician in methods of alleviating systems of illness that may not be part of his/her personal experience learned to utilize life's obstacles for growth and development. when, through understanding trial and error, and obstacle, problem or illness is overcome and a new experience of benefit is born out of an old problem, true healing has taken place. When such an individual extends his/her healing experience to others to help guide them through what they have experienced, a healer is created. The process to is continual. as a the healer helps to guide others he/she too is guided from 12 worked on by Queen Afua. she was about to apply a healing agent to my body when right before the applications the congestion in my chest began to break up and disperse. this was quite an extraordinary experience, i might add.

Sacred Woman: A Guide to Healing the Feminine Body, Mind, and Spirit by Queen Afua

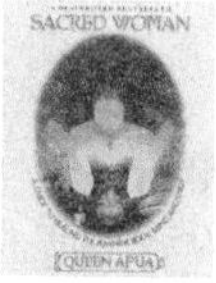

Queen Afua is a nationally renowned herbalist, natural health expert, and dedicated healer of women's bodies and women's souls who practices a uniquely Afrocentric spirituality. Her classic bestseller, Heal Thyself, forever changed the way African Americans practice holistic health. Now, with Sacred Woman, she takes us on a transforming journey of physical and ancestral healing that will restore the magnificence of our spirits through sacred initiation..

How to Eat to Live by Elijah Muhammad

How to eat and live a healthy life.

The Way of the Superior Man: A Spiritual Guide to Mastering the Challenges of Women, Work, and Sexual Desire by David Deida

The Ultimate Spiritual Guide for Men

In The Way of the Superior Man, David Deida explores the most important issues in men's lives—from career and family to women and intimacy to love and spirituality and relationships—to offer a practical guidebook for living a masculine life of integrity, authenticity, and freedom. Join this bestselling author and internationally renowned expert on sexual spirituality for straightforward advice, empowering skills, body practices, and more to help you realize a life of fulfillment, immediately and without compromise.

The Secret (The Secret, #1) by Rhonda Byrne

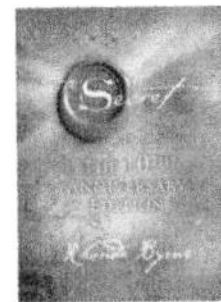

The Secret's 10th Anniversary Edition includes a new foreword by Rhonda Byrne, and 10 of the most life-changing insights she's had over the last 10 years of practicing and living The Secret every day. The 10 insights alone will accelerate your understanding and mastery of the law of attraction.

A Macat analysis of Frantz Fanon's Black Skin, White Masks by Rachele Dini

Frantz Fanon's Black Skin, White Masks offers a radical analysis of the psychological effects of colonization on the colonized. Born in 1925 on the island of Martinique—at the time a French colony—Fanon witnessed first hand the abuses of white colonizers and the system's effects on his country. His revulsion was only confirmed later in life when he worked as a psychiatrist in Algeria, another French colony.

Conscious Capitalism: Liberating the Heroic Spirit of Business by John E. Mackey

In this book, Whole Foods Market cofounder John Mackey and professor and Conscious Capitalism, Inc. cofounder Raj Sisodia argue for the inherent good of both business and capitalism. Featuring some of today's best-known companies, they illustrate how these two forces can—and do—work most powerfully to create value for all stakeholders: including customers, employees, suppliers, investors, society, and the environment.

Contagious: Why Things Catch On by Jonah Berger

If you've wondered why certain stories get shared, e-mails get forwarded, or videos go viral, Contagious explains why, and shows how to leverage these concepts to craft contagious content. This book provides a set of specific, actionable techniques for helping information spread - for designing messages, advertisements, and information that people will share. Whether you're a manager at a big company, a small business owner trying to boost awareness, a politician running for office, or a health official trying to get the word out, Contagious will show you how to make your product or idea catch on.

Creative Selection: Inside Apple's Design Process During the Golden Age of Steve Jobs by Ken Kocienda

An insider's account of Apple's creative process during the golden years of Steve Jobs.

Hundreds of millions of people use Apple products every day; several thousand work on Apple's campus in Cupertino, California; but only a handful sit at the drawing board. Creative Selection recounts the life of one of the few who worked behind the scenes, a highly-respected software engineer who worked in the final years the Steve Jobs era--the Golden Age of Apple.

Culture Vultures by Kenyatta Khari Griggs

Culture Vultures is an inside look at the creative and business genius behind some of America's greatest talents and fashion lines. Through a series of candid interviews over the span of 10 years, Kenyatta Griggs ask compelling and insightful questions that will help shed light on the music mogul, the father, and the man better known as Dame Dash.

Fooled by Randomness: The Hidden Role of Chance in Life and in the Markets by Nassim Nicholas Taleb

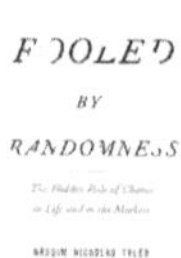

Fooled by Randomness is a standalone book in Nassim Nicholas Taleb's landmark Incerto series, an investigation of opacity, luck, uncertainty, probability, human error, risk, and decision-making in a world we don't understand. The other books in the series are The Black Swan, Antifragile,and The Bed of Procrustes.

I Didn't Do It for You: How the World Betrayed a Small African Nation by Michela Wrong

Scarred by decades of conflict and occupation, the craggy African nation of Eritrea has weathered the world's longest-running guerrilla war. The dogged determination that secured victory against Ethiopia, its giant neighbor, is woven into the national psyche, the product of cynical foreign interventions. Fascist Italy wanted Eritrea as the springboard for a new, racially pure Roman empire; Britain sold off its industry for scrap; the United States needed a base for its state-of-the-art spy station; and the Soviet Union used it as a pawn in a proxy war.

Invisible Influence: The Hidden Forces that Shape Behavior by Jonah Berger

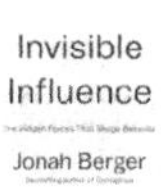

The New York Times bestselling author of Contagious explores the subtle, secret influences that affect the decisions we make—from what we buy, to the careers we choose, to what we eat—in this fascinating and groundbreaking work.

Law and Economics of Vertical Integration and Control by Roger D. Blair

Law and Economics of Vertical Integration and Control focuses on the processes, methodologies, and approaches involved in the law and economics of vertical integration and control.

Manchild in the Promised Land by Claude Brown

Manchild in the Promised Land is indeed one of the most remarkable autobiographies of our time. This thinly fictionalized account of Claude Brown's childhood as a hardened, streetwise criminal trying to survive the toughest streets of Harlem has been heralded as the definitive account of everyday life for the first generation of African Americans raised in the Northern ghettos of the 1940s and 1950s.

Message to the Blackman in America by Elijah Muhammad

Originally published: Chicago: Muhammad's Temple No. 2, 1965.

No Man Is an Island by Thomas Merton

Here, in one of his most popular of his more than thirty books, Thomas Merton provides further meditations on the spiritual life in sixteen thoughtful essays, beginning with his classic treatise "Love Can Be Kept Only by Being Given Away." This sequel to Seeds of Contemplation provides fresh insight into Merton's favorite topics of silence and solitude, while also underscoring the importance of community and the deep connectedness to others that is the inevitable basis of the spiritual life—whether one lives in solitude or in the midst of a crowd.

Originals: How Non-Conformists Move the World by Adam M. Grant

In Originals the author addresses the challenge of improving the world from the perspective of becoming original: choosing to champion novel ideas and values that go against the grain, battle conformity, and buck outdated traditions. How can we originate new ideas, policies, and practices without risking it all?

Political Economy: A Comparative Approach by Barry Clark

In this revised edition of the widely used and comprehensive overview of political/economic thought, political theory, sociology, and philosophy are integrated with economic analysis. Clark offers an introduction to the method and history of political economy, along with comparative studies of classical liberalism, radicalism, conservatism, and modern liberalism. Various issues such as the role of government, inflation and unemployment, poverty and inequality, and education, culture, and gender, are given a comparative analysis from the perspectives of the four major economic ideologies, and contemporary debates are traced back to their origins in the European industrialization process.

Power vs. Force by David R. Hawkins

David R. Hawkins details how anyone may resolve the most crucial of all human dilemmas: how to instantly determine the truth or falsehood of any statement or supposed fact. Dr. Hawkins, who worked as a "healing psychiatrist" during his long and distinguished career, uses theoretical concepts from particle physics, nonlinear dynamics, and chaos theory to support his study of human behavior. This is a fascinating work that will intrigue readers from all walks of life!

PowerNomics : The National Plan to Empower Black America by Claud Anderson

PowerNomics: The National Plan to Empower Black America is a five-year plan to make Black America a prosperous and empowered race that is self-sufficient and competitive as a group by the year 2005. In this book, Dr. Anderson obliterates the myths and illusions of black progress and brings together data and information from many different sources to construct a framework for solutions to the dilemma of Black America. In PowerNomics: The National Plan, Dr. Anderson proposes new principles, strategies and concepts that show blacks a new way to see, think, and behave in race matters. The new mind set prepares blacks to take strategic steps to create a new reality for their race. It offers guidance to others who support blacks self-sufficiency.

Purple Cow: Transform Your Business by Being Remarkable by Seth Godin

In Purple Cow, Seth Godin urges you to put a Purple Cow into everything you build, and everything you do, to create something truly noticeable. It's a manifesto for marketers who want to help create products that are worth marketing in the first place.

The Art & Science of Respect: A Memoir by James Prince by James Prince

For decades, serial entrepreneur James Prince presided over Rap-A-Lot Records, one of the first and most successful independent rap labels. In his memoir, he explains how he earned his reputation as one of the most respected men in Hip Hop. By staying true to his three principles of heart, loyalty, and commitment, and an unwavering faith in God, he has defeated many adversaries. Whether battling the systemic cycle of poverty, record label executives, boxing promoters, or corrupt

DEA agents, Prince has always emerged victorious.

Revolutionary Suicide by Huey P. Newton

Eloquently tracing the birth of a revolutionary, Huey P. Newton's famous and oft-quoted autobiography is as much a manifesto as a portrait of the inner circle of America's Black Panther Party. From Newton's impoverished childhood on the streets of Oakland to his adolescence and struggles with the system, from his role in the Black Panthers to his solitary confinement in the Alameda County Jail, Revolutionary Suicide is smart, unrepentant, and thought-provoking in its portrayal of inspired radicalism.

Rework by Jason Fried

Rework shows you a better, faster, easier way to succeed in business. Read it and you'll know why plans are actually harmful, why you don't need outside investors, and why you're better off ignoring the competition. The truth is, you need less than you think. You don't need to be a workaholic. You don't need to staff up. You don't need to waste time on paperwork or meetings. You don't even need an office. Those are all just excuses.

Rich Dad, Poor Dad by Robert T. Kiyosaki

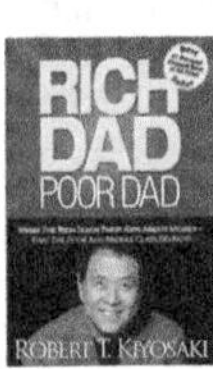

In Rich Dad Poor Dad, the #1 Personal Finance book of all time, Robert Kiyosaki shares the story of his two dad: his real father, whom he calls his 'poor dad,' and the father of his best friend, the man who became his mentor and his 'rich dad.' One man was well educated and an employee all his life, the other's education was "street smarts" over traditional classroom education and he took the path of entrepreneurship...a road that led him to become one of the wealthiest men in Hawaii. Robert's poor dad struggled financially all his life, and these two dads—these very different points of view of money, investing, and employment—shaped Robert's thinking about money.

Seize the Time: The Story of the Black Panther Party and Huey P. Newton by Bobby Seale

Sieze The Time is Bobby Seale's, a longtime activist and co-founder of The Black Panther Party, riveting first-person account on the evolution of The Party as a national organization. In the words of Seale the book "...continues to have a universal apppeal as an account

of an oppressed people's struggle for human liberation."

Seven Thousand Ways to Listen: Staying Close to What Is Sacred by Mark Nepo

In Seven Thousand Ways to Listen, Nepo offers ancient and contemporary practices to help us stay close to what is sacred. In this beautifully written spiritual memoir, Nepo explores the transformational journey with his characteristic insight and grace. He unfolds the many gifts and challenges of deep listening as we are asked to reflect on the life we are given. A moving exploration of self and our relationship to others and the world around us, Seven Thousand Ways to Listen unpacks the many ways we are called to redefine ourselves and to name what is meaningful as we move through the changes that come from experience and aging and the challenge of surviving loss.

Shoe Dog: A Memoir by the Creator of NIKE by Phil Knight

In this candid and riveting memoir, for the first time ever, Nike founder and CEO Phil Knight shares the inside story of the company's early days as an intrepid start-up and its evolution into one of the world's most iconic, game-changing, and profitable brands.

Steve Jobs by Walter Isaacson

Based on more than forty interviews with Jobs conducted over two years—as well as interviews with more than a hundred family members, friends, adversaries, competitors, and colleagues—Walter Isaacson has written a riveting story of the roller-coaster life and searingly intense personality of a creative entrepreneur whose passion for perfection and ferocious drive revolutionized six industries: personal computers, animated movies, music, phones, tablet computing, and digital publishing.

The Art of Seduction by Robert Greene

The Art of Seduction is a masterful synthesis of the work of thinkers such as Freud, Ovid, Kierkegaard, and Einstein, as well as the achievements of the greatest seducers throughout history. Twenty-four maneuvers will guide readers through the seduction process, providing cunning, amoral instructions for and analysis of this fascinating, all-pervasive form of power. Just as beautifully packaged and every bit as essential as The 48 Laws of Power, The Art of Seduction is an indispensable primer of persuasion and offers the best lessons on how to take what you want from whomever you want or how to prevent yourself from being taken.

The Art of War by Sun Tzu

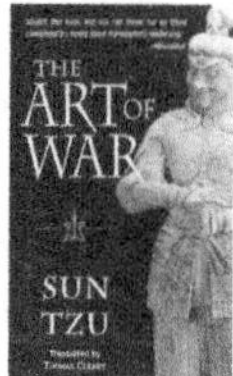

Twenty-Five Hundred years ago, Sun Tzu wrote this classic book of military strategy based on Chinese warfare and military thought. Since that time, all levels of military have used the teaching on Sun Tzu to warfare and civilization have adapted these teachings for use in politics, business and everyday life. The Art of War is a book which should be used to gain advantage of opponents in the boardroom and battlefield alike.

The I Ching or Book of Changes by Anonymous

The I Ching, or Book of Changes, is one of the 1st efforts of the human mind to place itself within the universe. It has exerted a living influence in China for 3000 years and interest in it has spread in the West. Set down in the dawn of history as a book of oracles, the Book of Changes deepened in meaning when ethical values were attached to the oracular pronouncements; it became a book of wisdom, eventually one of the Five Classics of Confucianism, and provided the common source for both Confucianist and Taoist philosophy.

The Beautiful Struggle: A Father, Two Sons and an Unlikely Road to Manhood by Ta-Nehisi Coates

The Beautiful Struggle follows their divergent paths through this turbulent period, and their father's steadfast efforts assisted by mothers, teachers, and a body of myths, histories, and rituals conjured from the past to meet the needs of a troubled present to keep them whole in a world that seemed bent on their destruction. With a remarkable ability to reimagine both the lost world of his fathers generation and the terrors and wonders of his own youth, Coates offers readers a small and beautiful epic about boys trying to become men in black America and beyond.

The Fire Next Time by James Baldwin

A national bestseller when it first appeared in 1963, The Fire Next Time galvanized the nation and gave passionate voice to the emerging civil rights movement. At once a powerful evocation of James Baldwin's early life in Harlem and a disturbing examination of the consequences of racial injustice, the book is an intensely personal and provocative document. It consists of two "letters," written on the occasion of the centennial of the Emancipation Proclamation, that exhort Americans, both black and white, to attack the terrible legacy of racism. Described by The New York Times Book Review as "sermon, ultimatum, confession, deposition, testament, and chronicle...all presented in searing, brilliant prose," The

Fire Next Time stands as a classic of our literature.

The Four: The Hidden DNA of Amazon, Apple, Facebook, and Google by Scott Galloway

Amazon, Apple, Facebook, and Google are the four most influential companies on the planet. Just about everyone thinks they know how they got there. Just about everyone is wrong.

For all that's been written about the Four over the last two decades, no one has captured their power and staggering success as insightfully as Scott Galloway.

Invisible Man by Ralph Ellison

First published in 1952 and immediately hailed as a masterpiece, Invisible Man is one of those rare novels that have changed the shape of American literature. For not only does Ralph Ellison's nightmare journey across the racial divide tell unparalleled truths about the nature of bigotry and its effects on the minds of both victims and perpetrators, it gives us an entirely new model of what a novel can be.

The Isis Papers: The Keys to the Colors by Frances Cress Welsing

A collection of 25 essays examining the neuroses of white supremacy.

The Lost Book of Enoch by David Humphreys

Though widely read by early Christians, the book of Enoch was banned by the church in the fourth century and considered lost for 1,600 years. A mention of it in the New Testament led 19th-century scholars to a manuscript of the Enoch story in Hebrew and Aramaic verse, and a theological study of the manuscript in English followed in 1912. Yet it too eventually disappeared from public view. This edition of the lost biblical book is re-written in contemporary English and recounts the apocalyptic vision revealed to Enoch, the father of Methuselah, when he was taken to heaven by archangels who showed him the future of mankind as he looked down upon the world.

The One Device: The Secret History of the iPhone by Brian Merchant

We know the iPhone as the device that transformed our world, changing everything from how we talk to each other and do business, to how we exercise, travel, shop, and watch TV. But packed within its slim profile is the fascinating, untold story of scientific, technological, and business breakthroughs--global in scope, sometimes centuries in the making, and coming from vastly different disciplines--that enabled Apple to create the most profitable product in history.

The Peebles Principles by R. Donahue Peebles

Part The Art of the Deal and part Why Should White Guys Have All the Fun, The Peebles Principles distills the lessons Mr. Peebles has learned on his journey from congressional page to CEO of the largest black-owned real-estate development firm in the nation. These crisp, straightforward principles can help any motivated entrepreneur go from dirt poor to filthy rich in a hurry.

Some lessons are motivational and inspirational; many are hardball business how-to's that apply in any industry and any type of transaction.

The Richest Man in Babylon by George S. Clason

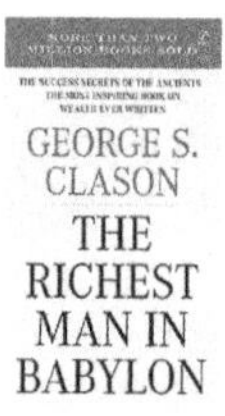

by the famous "Babylonian parables," hailed as the greatest of all inspirational works on the subject of thrift, financial planning, and personal wealth. In language as simple as that found in the Bible, these fascinating and informative stories set you on a sure path to prosperity and its accompanying joys. Acclaimed as a modern-day classic, this celebrated bestseller offers an understanding of—and a solution to—your personal financial problems that will guide you through a lifetime. This is the book that holds the secrets to keeping your money—and making more.

The Second Sex by Simone de Beauvoir

Newly translated and unabridged in English for the first time, Simone de Beauvoir's masterwork is a powerful analysis of the Western notion of "woman," and a groundbreaking exploration of inequality and otherness. This long-awaited new edition reinstates significant portions of the original French text that were cut in the first English translation. Vital and groundbreaking, Beauvoir's pioneering and impressive text remains as pertinent today as it was back then, and will continue to provoke and inspire generations of men and women to come.

The Spook Who Sat by the Door by Sam Greenlee

This book is both a satire of the civil rights problems in the United States in the late 60s and a serious attempt to focuses on the issue of black militancy.

The Wretched of the Earth by Frantz Fanon

The Wretched of the Earth is a brilliant analysis of the psychology of the colonized and their path to liberation. Bearing singular insight into the rage and frustration of colonized peoples, and the role of violence in effecting historical change, the book incisively attacks the twin perils of post-independence colonial politics: the disenfranchisement of the masses by the elites on the one hand, and intertribal and interfaith animosities on the other.

The 22 Immutable Laws of Marketing: Violate Them at Your Own Risk by Al Ries

As Al Ries and Jack Trout—the world-renowned marketing consultants and bestselling authors of Positioning—note, you can build an impressive airplane, but it will never leave the ground if you ignore the laws of physics, especially gravity. Why then, they ask, shouldn't there also be laws of marketing that must be followed to launch and maintain winning brands? In The 22 Immutable Laws of Marketing, Ries and Trout offer a compendium of twenty-two innovative rules for understanding and succeeding in the international marketplace. From the Law of Leadership, to The Law of the Category, to The Law of the Mind, these valuable insights stand the test of time and present a clear path to successful products. Violate them at your own risk.

The 22 Immutable Laws of Branding: How to Build a Product or Service Into a World-Class Brand by Al Ries

The only way to stand out in today's -- and tomorrow's -- cluttered marketplace is to build your product or service into a brand. Think Nike, Starbuck's, Xerox, and Kleenex, and you're thinking brands in the biggest and most lucrative sense. In The 22 Immutable Laws of Branding, marketing guru Al Ries, together with Laura Ries, has put together the authoritative work on brands and branding -- organized in a short, pithy book that can be read and digested in as brief a time as an airplane ride.

Think and Grow Rich by Napoleon Hill

This is the original 1937 version of Napoleon Hill's Classic Book: Think and Grow Rich. To the greatest extent possible, the text and formatting have been kept exactly the same as in the original release with the exception of some minor formatting changes.

Three Magic Words by Uell S. Andersen

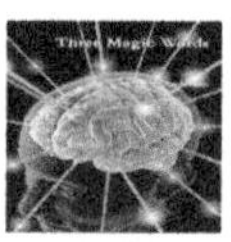

As author Uell Stanley Andersen (1917- 1986) will show you in the pages of "Three Magic Words," you will learn of the unlimited power that is yours, in you. You will learn how you can turn this power to work for you, here on earth, to make your life majestic and overflowing with good. Three Magic Words is not a religion or a sect or a society. In its entirety it is a series of essays aimed at revealing to you your power over all things. You will learn that there is only one mover in all creation and that mover is thought. You will learn that there is only one creator and that creator is the Universal Subconscious Mind, or God. You will learn that this creator creates for you exactly what you think, and you will be shown how you can control your thoughts, not only to obtain answers to your problems but to create in your experience exactly what you desire.

Vertical Integration and Technological Innovation: A Transaction Cost Approach by Yeong Heok Lee

Originally published in 1994 this volume investigates the relationship between a firm's decision to integrate vertically and its research and development (R & D) strategy. Literature on vertical integration is reviewed and a framework presented to analyze the costs and benefits of vertical integration. The theoretical basis for the proposed hypostheses is investigated and the hypotheses tested empirically.

Tools of Titans: The Tactics, Routines, and Habits of Billionaires, Icons, and World-Class Performers by Timothy Ferriss

From the author:

"This book contains the distilled tools, tactics, and 'inside baseball' you won't find anywhere else. It also includes new tips from past guests, and life lessons from new 'guests' you haven't met.

We Were Eight Years in Power: An American Tragedy by Ta-Nehisi Coates

"We were eight years in power" was the lament of Reconstruction-era black politicians as the American experiment in multiracial democracy ended with the return of white supremacist rule in the South. Now Ta-Nehisi Coates explores the tragic echoes of that history in our own time: the unprecedented election of a black president followed by a vicious backlash that fueled the election of the man Coates argues is America's "first white president."

The 1% Rule: How to Fall in Love with the Process and Achieve Your Wildest Dreams by Tommy Baker

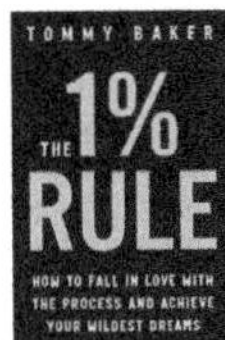

The 1% Rule was designed to answer three core questions:

Why do some people seem to achieve massive success in everything they do, while others can't even get out of their own way?

What separates those who get excited and inspired for a season, a quarter, a month or a week – and those who are consistently on fire?

What are the core principles, mindsets, habits and rituals of those who execute ruthlessly, and those who sit on the sidelines pondering?

2022 Anunnaki Code: End Of The World Or Their Return To Earth ?: Ulema Book Of Parallel Dimension, Extraterrestrials And Akashic Records by Jean-Maximillien De La Croix de Lafayette

This remarkable book has many facets, and is so extremely rich in content that trying to introduce it is not an easy task. The material is unique, to start with. Most of it has been learned from sources that are totally out of reach for the average reader - and even for many scholars.

Some of this material was hidden in the archives of museums, some written on tablets that have never been translated before, and some of it is oral knowledge that have never been given to a Westerner before. The author, Maximillien de Lafayette, have been so fortunate as to study with those who are the guardians of this knowledge in Lebanon, Egypt, Iraq, the islands of Arwad and Cyprus, and his travels even took him to the Far East, where he studied with Tibetan and Japanese teachers. This is the first time he is making use of this depot of knowledge, and we are very lucky to have access to it.

The 48 Laws of Power by Robert Greene
Soul on Ice by Eldridge Cleaver

This amoral, cunning, ruthless, and instructive book synthesizes the philosophies of Machiavelli, Sun Tzu, and Carl Von Clausewitz with the historical legacies of statesmen, warriors, seducers, and con men throughout the ages.

7

About the Author

Ash Exantus also known as Ash Cash is one of the leading personal finance experts in the U.S. Dubbed as the Hip-Hop Financial Motivator, Ash Cash uses a culturally responsive approach in teaching financial empowerment and entrepreneurship. He is also a best-selling author of six books including the Jay-Z inspired book "The Wake Up Call: Financial

Lessons Learned from 444." He is the founder and Chief Financial Educator at MindRight Money Management, a Financial Education and Media company that blends psychology and personal finance with music, pop culture and relevant news to help people manage their money better in order to live the life that they want. He is also a Financial teacher as well as a Leadership Council member of the World of Money Financial Institute, a 501(c)(3) non-profit organization whose mission is to empower youth with an immersive financial and technology education, creating financially responsible adults one child at a time.

www.IamAshCash.com

@IamAshCash @AshCashExantus

@IamAshCash linkedin.com/in/IamAshCash

Ash has established himself as a thought leader and trusted voice with Corporate America, Colleges, Churches, and Community based organizations. Through his message of fiscal responsibility, entrepreneurship, and wealth empowerment, he has become a regular speaker at national conferences across the country.

Above all of his credentials, accolades, and titles, Ash is simply known for helping people maximize their full potentials. You can also read more about Ash by visiting www.IamAshCash.com

Books By Ash Cash

The Wake Up Call

The Wake Up Call: Financial Inspiration Learned from 4:44 + A Step by Step Guide on How to Implement Each Financial Principle, is a book designed to teach African-Americans how to manage money more effectively and how to build generational wealth. Jay-Z's 4:44 is the blueprint to bridging the wealth gap & solving economic inequalities for African-Americans! Through deciphering all of the financial concepts delivered within the album, readers will be taught about:

- How to Build Credit to Use as Leverage • How to Spend Money Wisely
- Cooperative Economics and How to Start a Business
- Creating Multiple Streams of Income • How to Invest Money in Order For it To Grow
- How to Pass Down Wealth to the Next Generation

Mind Right, Money Right

Mind Right, Money Right: 10 Laws of Financial Freedom, is a book designed to teach you how to effectively manage your personal finances. It shows you how having the right mental attitude and with laser sharp focus, you can have anything you desire in life. It's an easy to read book that anyone, at any level, can understand. The book's aim is to teach you these 10 proven Laws of Financial Freedom using the stories of wealthy men and women who have used them. This book is especially geared towards anyone who is tired of having a dependency on money and is ready to take some practical steps in order to correct it. Money is power but knowing how to make it work for you is freedom; Mind Right, Money Right will teach you how.

Mind Right, Life Right

The Law of Attraction is arguably the most powerful law in the universe and over the past 10+ years many people have been realizing its power, especially with the introduction of The Secret. But what if I told you that it wasn't the only law? And if you only utilize the Law of Attraction you will be disappointed when your dreams aren't materializing? Mind Right, Life Right: Manifesting Your Dreams Through the Laws of the Universe is a book written to help those who are seeking true enlightenment, learn how to turn their dreams into reality. Through the nine Mindset Principles, readers will learn that the Law of Attraction is just a piece of the puzzle (although a big piece), and that if you combine this law with the other powerful principles that govern the universe, you can achieve ANYTHING you put your mind, grind and focus towards.

What the FICO

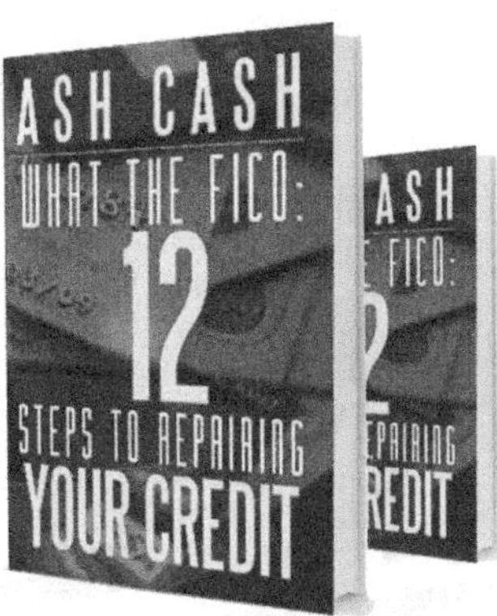

What the FICO: 12 Steps To Repairing Your Credit is the only credit repair book you'll ever need. It is a simple guide that will give you step-by-step instruction on how to go from bad to good credit in no time and minimal cost. If you follow these simple steps you are going to begin the journey of getting your credit and financial life back in order. This book is mainly for those who have tried to learn the credit game and have done so unsuccessfully but can also be used by those who are just starting out to get a better understanding of how to build a good credit history. - Learn your rights as a consumer and how to protect them - Learn how to remove negative items from your report (Even the ones you're responsible for) - Correct and remove errors and improve your credit score - Negotiate with creditors to reduce debt - Add positive information to your credit report - Re-Build a Solid Credit history

Taylor's Way

Have you ever spent time observing a child or group of children and how they conduct their young lives? The one thing you will immediately notice is that they live life by their instincts. They are enthusiastic, always eager to learn, curious, brave, and will try almost anything without hesitation. These characteristics and more are all the keys to happiness but unfortunately as we transition from childhood to adulthood we replace these natural instincts with what adults call "reality." As I watched my daughter Taylor grow, I began to realize that she had not been tainted by our ideas of "reality" and as a result was always happy and tended to get everything she wanted out of life effortlessly. Isn't that what we all want of our lives? In the following pages you will read in detail the valuable lessons I've learned from my three year old daughter. Each chapter illustrates through the eyes of a child how you can live a happier life the way it was intended for you to live! Life is abundant! Life is enjoyable! Life is exactly how you imagined it in your wildest dreams! Today is the day that you bring it back to that essence!

Making Sense of Kanye

Kanye West has become one of the most controversial artists of the 21st century. His antics often result in the questioning of his sanity and has many people wondering whether he is a master of publicity, who simply knows how to keep his name in the news or if he really needs professional help. Despite that, if we study the man himself and remove emotional reactions from what he says or does, there are many things we can learn from Donda Wests' son. Furthermore, if we take a deeper look into Kanye and his antics, we will see a bigger message as it relates to mental health and money. Making Sense of Kanye is a book designed to teach you how to obtain financial freedom, peace, love, and happiness and how to avoid (or cope with) societal pressures. Using Kanye Wests' misunderstood wisdom, we explore how many of his thoughts coincide with spiritual law and how we can use these laws to live a well-balanced life regardless of economic status. There is no doubt that Mr. West is a musical genius that can sometimes say the wrong things at the wrong time but can we open our minds and allow him to teach us some important aspects of life? This book will show you how!

The 21 Day Mind Right, Money Right Challenge

The 21 Day Mind Right, Money Right Challenge is a tool designed to help retrain your brain to effectively attract and attain the financial life you deserve. This is a 21 day challenge that takes you through 21 specific actions so you can renew your money mindset.Get Rid of Old Habits +Learn How Your Old Habits are Keeping You From Your AbundanceCreate Good Vibes Only +Understand the Importance of Clearing Your Mind of Negative ThoughtsChange Your Perspective on Money +Learn and understand that abundance is your birthright and with the right money attitudes you can have everything you want in life Understand The Importance of Meditation with a Quick Start Guide

Made in the USA
Middletown, DE
03 March 2024

50727745R00106